DMV Seminar
Band 11

Birkhäuser Verlag
Basel · Boston · Berlin

Tammo tom Dieck
Ian Hambleton

Surgery Theory and Geometry of Representations

1988

Birkhäuser Verlag
Basel · Boston · Berlin

Authors

T. tom Dieck
Mathematisches Institut der
Georg-August-Universität
Bunsenstrasse 3–5
D–3400 Göttingen

I. Hambleton
Dept. of Mathematics & Statistics
McMaster University
1280 Main Street West
Hamilton, Ontario
Canada L8S 4K1

The seminar was made possible through the support of the
Stiftung Volkswagenwerk

CIP-Kurztitelaufnahme der Deutschen Bibliothek

Surgery theory and geometry of representations / Tammo tom Dieck ; Ian Hambleton. –
Basel ; Boston ; Berlin : Birkhäuser, 1988
(DMV-Seminar ; Bd. 11)
ISBN 3-7643-2204-7 (Basel . . .) brosch.
ISBN 0-8176-2204-7 (Boston) brosch.
NE: Tom Dieck, Tammo [Mitverf.]; Hambleton, Ian [Mitverf.];
Deutsche Mathematiker-Vereinigung: DMV-Seminar

Printed in Germany
ISBN 3-7643-2204-7
ISBN 0-8176-2204-7

Contents

Preface

These notes were prepared for the DMV-Seminar held in Düsseldorf, Schloss Mickeln from June 28 to July 5, 1987. They consist of two parts which can be read independently. The reader is presumed to have a basic education in differential and algebraic topology.

Surgery theory is the basic tool for the investigation of differential and topological manifolds. A systematic development of the theory is a long and difficult task. The purpose of these notes is to describe simple examples and at the same time to give an introduction to some of the systematic parts of the theory.

The first part is concerned with examples. They are related to representations of finite groups and group actions on spheres, and are considered as a generalisation of the spherical space form problem.

The second part reviews the general setting of surgery theory and reports on the computation of the surgery abstraction groups.

Both parts present material not covered in any textbook and also give an introduction to the literature and areas of research.

1. REPRESENTATION FORMS AND HOMOTOPY REPRESENTATIONS.

Tammo tom Dieck

Mathematical Institute
Göttingen University
Fed. Rep. of Germany

Let G be a (finite) group. We consider group actions of G on spheres and spherelike spaces.

An orthogonal representation of G consists of a real vector space V with inner product $<-,->$ and an action $G \times V \to V$, $(g,v) \mapsto gv$ of G on V such that the left translations $l_g : v \mapsto gv$ are orthogonal linear maps. If we choose an orthonormal basis in V and express l_g as a matrix $A(g)$ with respect to this basis, then $g \mapsto A(g)$ is a homomorphism of G into the orthogonal group. Similarly, one has the notion of a unitary representation by using complex vector spaces and hermitian inner products.

1.1 Example. The cyclic group $\mathbb{Z}/m$ of order m will be identified with the group of m-th roots of unity in the circle group $S^1 = \{z \in \mathbb{C} \mid |z| = 1\}$. We have one-dimensional unitary representations

$$V_k : Z/m \times \mathbb{C} \mapsto \mathbb{C},\ (a,z) \mapsto a^k z \quad \text{for}$$
$$k = 0,1,\ldots,m-1.$$

1.2 Example. The dihedral group D_{2m} of order $2m$ is given by generators and relations as follows

$$D_{2m} = \langle A,B \mid A^m = 1 = B^2, BAB^{-1} = A^{-1} \rangle .$$

The element A generates a cyclic normal subgroup $\langle A \rangle$ of order m. We obtain orthogonal representations W_k on $\mathbb{C} = \mathbb{R}^2$ by specifying the left translations

$$l_A(Z) = \zeta^k z, \qquad \zeta = \exp(2\pi\, i/m)$$
$$l_B(z) = \bar{z}.$$

One verifies $l_B^{-1} l_A l_B = l_A^{-1}$ and shows that $z \mapsto \bar{z}$ is an isomorphism $W_k \to W_{-k}$ of representations. Thus it suffices to consider the cases $0 \leq k \leq [\frac{m}{2}]$.

Given orthogonal representations V and W of G one can form the <u>direct sum</u> $V \oplus W$, with group action $(g,(v,w)) \mapsto (gv,gw)$. A representation V is called <u>irreducible</u> if it has no G-invariant subspace W, $0 \neq W \neq V$. Each representation is a direct sum of irreducible representations. If $\mathrm{Irr}(G,\mathbb{R})$ is a complete set of pairwise non-isomorphic irreducible orthogonal representations and if we write nW for the n-fold direct sum of the representation W, then in an expression

$$V \cong \bigoplus_{W \in \mathrm{Irr}(G,\mathbb{R})} n(w)W \quad , \; n(w) \in \mathbb{Z}$$

the integers $n(W)$ are uniquely determined by W. The direct sum operation induces a commutative, associative composition law on the set of isomorphism classes of orthogonal representations. Let $RO(G)$ be the corresponding Grothendieck group. Tensor product of representations makes $RO(G)$ into a commutative ring, called the real <u>representation ring</u>. We are mainly concerned with its additive structure: It is the free abelian group on the set $\mathrm{Irr}(G,\mathbb{R})$. For unitary representations we use the notation $\mathrm{Irr}(G,\mathbb{C})$ for the set of irreducible representations and $R(G)$ for the complex representation ring. For basic facts about representations see BRÖCKER-TOM DIECK [1985], SERRE [1971].

1.3 Example. One has, see (1.1),

$$\mathrm{Irr}(\mathbb{Z}/m,\mathbb{C}) = \{V_o, V_1, \dots, V_{m-1}\}.$$

From $V_k \otimes_{\mathbb{C}} V_1 \cong V_{k+1}$ (indices mod m) one obtains the ring structure

$$R(\mathbb{Z}/m) \cong \mathbb{Z}[x]/(x^m-1),$$

where x corresponds to V_1.

1.4 Example. Let G be abelian. A unitary irreducible representation is one-dimensional. There are $|G|$ different irreducible representations . ($|G|$ order of G.) The set $\check{G} = \mathrm{Irr}(G,\mathbb{C})$ becomes a group with tensor product of representations as multiplication (the dual group, the character group). The representation ring RG is isomorphic to the group ring $\mathbb{Z}\check{G}$.

Let $S(V)$ be the unit sphere in an orthogonal or unitary representations of G. There is an induced G-action on $S(V)$. We call $S(V)$ a representation sphere. Let H be a subgroup of G (notation $H \subset G$). The H-fixed point set

$$V^H = \{x \in V \mid hx = x \text{ for all } h \in H\}$$

is a linear subspace and because of

$$S(V)^H = S(V^H)$$

the fixed point sets in representation spheres are always spheres (or empty).

Given spaces X and Y one can form the join $X * Y$. This is the quotient space of $X \times [0,1] \times Y$ with respect to the relations

$$(x,o,y) \sim (x',o,y)$$
$$(x,1,y) \sim (x,1,y').$$

Intuitively, in the join each point of X and each point of Y are connected by a unit interval. If X and Y are G-spaces, then $X * Y$ inherits a G-action from $(g,(x,t,y)) \mapsto (gx,t,gy)$. The join operation is a functorial construction: If $f : X \to X'$ and $h : Y \to Y'$ are G-maps there is an induced G-map $f * h : (x,t,y) \longmapsto (fx,t,hy)$. If f and h are G-homotopy equivalences so is $f * h$. For representation spheres one has a G-homeomorphism

1.5 $$S(V \oplus W) \cong S(V) * S(W).$$

The significance of this G-homeomorphism is that it provides a purely homotopical construction for the unit sphere in a direct sum. Therefore this construction can be generalized to other group actions as we will see in a moment. For basic vocabulary and facts about group actions see TOM DIECK [1987].

The Clifford-Klein space form problem asks for the determination of the compact Riemannian manifolds with constant positive curvature. If M is such a space form one can show that the universal covering $\tilde{M}$ is isometric to a standard sphere such that the decktransformation group G acts via orthogonal maps. (See WOLF [1967], p. 69). Since G must act freely in this case the space form problem amounts to a problem in representation theory: Classify free representations (i.e. representations with free action on the unit sphere). The groups which can have free representations are very restricted. In particular one has

1.6 Proposition. Let G be a finite group which admits a fixed point free representation over $\mathbb{R}$ or $\mathbb{C}$. If H is a subgroup of order pq in G, for primes p and q, then H is cyclic.

Proof. Let V be a free representation and let $H \subset G$ be a non-trivial subgroup. The vector $\sum_{h\in H} hv$ is contained in V^H and is therefore the zero vector. Let H be non-cyclic of order pq.

Let $S_1,\dots,S_k$ be the set of proper subgroup of H. Then each S_i is cyclic of order $1,p$, or q. If $1 \neq h \in H$, then h belongs to precisely one of the S_i. The identity

$$\sum_{i=1}^{k} \sum_{s \in S_i} sv = 0$$

can be written $\sum_{1 \neq h \in H} hv + kv = 0.$
Subtracting $\sum hv = 0$ yields $(k-1)v = 0$, hence $v = 0$ for all $v \in V$. □

If every subgroup of order pq of G is cyclic we say that G satisfies the pq-condition. The case $p = q$ is allowed.

We now consider more general group actions on spheres than representations. But we want to retain some of the geometry of a representation sphere.

A smooth representation form of G is a C^∞-differentiable action $G \times M \to M$ on a differentiable manifold M such that for all subgroups H of G the fixed set M^H is homeomorphic to a sphere (or empty). We are thus allowing differentiable structures on M^H which differ from the structure on the standard sphere. A topological representation form of G is a continuous action of G on a topological manifold M such that for all subgroups H of G the fixed set M^H is homeomorphic to a sphere.

A basic topological invariant of a representation form is its G-homotopy type. We therefore consider the homotopical analogue of a representation form.

A homotopy representation of G is a G-complex X with the following properties: For each $H \subset G$ the fixed point set X^H has the homotopy type of a sphere $S^{n(H)-1}$ and X^H is a complex of dimension $n(H)-1$. (We set $n(H) = 0$ if X^H is empty.) If H is conjugate to K in G, in symbols $H \sim K$, then $n(H) = n(K)$. Let (H) denote the conjugacy class of the subgroup H, let $\Phi(G)$ denote the set of conjugacy classes and let $C(G) = C(\Phi(G),\mathbb{Z})$ be the ring of all functions $\Phi(G) \to \mathbb{Z}$.

A homotopy representation X leads to a function $\mathrm{Dim}\, X \in C(G)$,

$$\mathrm{Dim}\, X : (H) \mapsto n(H),$$

called the <u>dimension function</u> of G. If X and Y are homotopy representations, then $X * Y$ is again a homotopy representation. We have

1.7 $$\mathrm{Dim}\,(X * Y) = \mathrm{Dim}\, X + \mathrm{Dim}\, Y.$$

A representation sphere $S(V)$ of an orthogonal representation V may be considered as a smooth representation form and as a homotopy representation. The latter requires an equivariant triangulation of $S(V)$.

We remark that the actual cellular structure of a homotopy representation is irrelevant. For this reason we also call a space "homotopy representation" if it has the G-homotopy type of a homotopy representation as defined above.

The relation (1.7) is the reason for using $n(H)-1$ instead of $n(H)$ in the definition. Also note that

$$\mathrm{Dim}\, S(V)\,(H) = \dim_{\mathbb{R}} V^H,$$

where $\dim_{\mathbb{R}}$ denotes the dimension of a real vector space. A homotopy representation is called, by abuse of language, <u>linear</u> if it has the G-homotopy type of a representation sphere. Likewise, we call a dimension function linear, if it is the dimension function of some representation sphere.

The join operation induces on the set of G-homotopy types of homotopy representations a commutative and associative composition law. Let $V^{\infty}(G)$ be the corresponding Grothendieck group. This group is called the <u>homotopy representation group</u> of G. A homotopy representation is called <u>finite</u> if it is G-homotopy equivalent to a finite G-complex. Let $V(G)$ denote the homotopy representation group of finite homotopy representations. There is a canonical homomorphism $V(G) \rightarrow V^{\infty}(G)$, the identity on representatives.

It can be shown to be injective; see TOM DIECK - PETRIE [1978], where homotopy representations were introduced. Similarly, by (1.5), there is defined a canonical homomorphism $RO(G) \to V(G)$ by assigning to each representation V its sphere SV; let $TO(G)$ be its kernel and $JO(G)/TO(G) \to V(G)$ the induced injection. It can be shown that the group $TO(G)$ consists of differences $V - W$ of stably homotopy equivalent representations V,W. Representations V and W are called <u>stably homotopy equivalent</u> if there exists a representation U such that $S(V \oplus U)$ and $S(W \oplus U)$ are G-homotopy equivalent.

There exist many variants of the groups $V^{\infty}(G)$ and $V(G)$. Let F be a set of subgroups of G which is closed under conjugation and intersection. Consider only homotopy representations X with isotropy groups in F. This property is preserved under joins. Therefore we have a Grothendieck group $V^{\infty}(G,F)$ of such homotopy representations.

A representation form M is called a <u>space form</u> if it carries a free action. Space forms are thus generalisations of Clifford-Klein space forms.

The relation (1.7) shows that taking dimension functions induces a homomorphism

1.8 $\quad \mathrm{Dim} : V^{\infty}(G) \to C(G).$

We denote its kernel by $v^{\infty}(G)$. We have similar kernels $jO(G) \subset JO(G)$ and $v(G) \subset V(G)$. For more details about homotopy representations see TOM DIECK [1987], II.10.

One of the basic problems which will be addressed in these lectures is the following.

<u>1.9 Problem.</u> Which homotopy representations can be realized by smooth representation forms?

This problem will be attacked by surgery theory. It turns out that the geometry of smooth representation forms imposes several restrictions on the homotopy types - not every homotopy representation can be realized.

The method of surgery theory uses as an input "normal maps".

In our context normal maps appear as "tangential structures" on homotopy representations - in the following form.

Let X be a homotopy representation of G. A <u>tangential</u> structure on X is a commutative diagram

1.10
$$\begin{array}{ccc} TM \oplus k\varepsilon & \xrightarrow{F} & \eta \\ \downarrow & & \downarrow p \\ M & \xrightarrow{f} & X \end{array}$$

consisting of the following data and having the following properties:

(i) M is a smooth G-manifold with tangent bundle TM.

(ii) $k\varepsilon$ is the trivial k-dimensional bundle with trivial action.

(iii) f is a G-map.

(iv) η is a G-vector bundle over X and F a G-vector bundle map over f.

(v) $\mathrm{Iso}(M) = \mathrm{Iso}(X)$. (Iso = set of isotopy groups.)

(vi) For $H \in \mathrm{Iso}(M)$, the H-fixed points M^H and X^H have the same dimension and $f^H : M^H \to X^H$ has degree one.

Condition (vi) requires M^H and X^H to be oriented in order that the notion of degree is well-defined.

<u>1.11 Example.</u> A natural candidate for η is the trivial bundle. For a sphere we have $TS^n \oplus \varepsilon = (n+1)\varepsilon$.

The method of surgery theory is concerned with the problem of changing f into an equivariant homotopy equivalence. One begins with the fixed point sets (if there are any) and then adds one orbit bundle at a time. Later we shall be more precise about this procedure.

I shall describe in these notes three methods for the construction of tangential structures:

(i) Construction of manifolds from representations.

(ii) Manifolds given by equations (algebraic varieties).

(iii) Construction of manifolds by transversality.

2. Homotopy representations with free action.

We describe the homotopy theory which is relevant for the space form problem. Let X be a homotopy representation for G with free action. Let X be $(n-1)$-dimensional. Assume that the action of G on $H_{n-1}(X;\mathbb{Z}) \cong \mathbb{Z}$ is trivial; (we then say that the G-action preserves the orientation). The cellular chain complex C_* of X leads to an exact sequence

2.1
$$\begin{array}{ccccccccccccc} 0 & \to & \mathbb{Z} & \xrightarrow{i} & C_{n-1} & \to & C_{n-2} & \to & \cdots & \to & C_0 & \xrightarrow{\varepsilon} \mathbb{Z} & \to 0 \\ & & \| & & & & & & & & & \| & \\ & & H_{n-1}(X) & & & & & & & & & H_0(X) & \end{array}$$

with free $\mathbb{Z}G$-modules $C_0,\dots,C_{n-1}$. This is the beginning of a free resolution of the $\mathbb{Z}G$-module $\mathbb{Z}$ in the sense of homological algebra. We can splice such sequences; we use $C_0 \xrightarrow{\varepsilon} \mathbb{Z} \xrightarrow{i} C_{n-1}$. There results a free resolution of $\mathbb{Z}$ which is periodic of period n. The cohomology groups of the complex

$$\mathrm{Hom}_{\mathbb{Z}G}(C_0,\mathbb{Z}) \to \mathrm{Hom}_{\mathbb{Z}G}(C_1,\mathbb{Z}) \to \mathrm{Hom}_{\mathbb{Z}G}(C_2,\mathbb{Z}) \to \cdots$$

are called the cohomology groups $H^k(G;\mathbb{Z})$ of the group G. The periodicity of the resolution shows that the cohomology groups are periodic:

2.2 $\qquad H^k(G;\mathbb{Z}) \cong H^{k+n}(G;\mathbb{Z}) \qquad , k > 0.$

We say that G has <u>periodic cohomology of period</u> n if (2.2) holds.

<u>2.3 Proposition</u>. $H^n(G;\mathbb{Z}) \cong \mathbb{Z}/|G|$.

<u>Proof</u>. The sequence

$$\mathrm{Hom}_{\mathbb{Z}G}(C_1,\mathbb{Z}) \leftarrow \mathrm{Hom}_{\mathbb{Z}G}(C_0,\mathbb{Z}) \leftarrow \mathrm{Hom}_{\mathbb{Z}G}(\mathbb{Z},\mathbb{Z}) \leftarrow 0$$

is exact. Therefore $H^n(G,\mathbb{Z})$ is the cokernel of

$$i^* : \mathrm{Hom}_{\mathbb{Z}G}(C_{n-1},\mathbb{Z}) \longrightarrow \mathrm{Hom}_{\mathbb{Z}G}(\mathbb{Z},\mathbb{Z}) \cong \mathbb{Z} .$$

Note that $i : \mathbb{Z} \to C_{n-1}$ is an inclusion of a $\mathbb{Z}$-direct summand since the image of $C_{n-1} \to C_{n-2}$ is a free abelian group. The next result implies (2.3). □

<u>2.4 Lemma</u>. Let F be a free (or projective) $\mathbb{Z}G$-module and let $i : \mathbb{Z} \to F$ be a $\mathbb{Z}G$-linear inclusion of a $\mathbb{Z}$-direct summand. then the cokernel of $i^* : \mathrm{Hom}_{\mathbb{Z}G}(F,\mathbb{Z}) \to \mathrm{Hom}_{\mathbb{Z}G}(\mathbb{Z},\mathbb{Z})$ is isomorphic to $\mathbb{Z}/|G|$.

<u>Proof</u>. Given a $\mathbb{Z}$-linear homomorphism $f : B \to C$ between $\mathbb{Z}G$-modules B and C we let

$$N(f)(b) = \sum_{g\in G} gf(g^{-1}b)$$

be the associated $\mathbb{Z}G$-linear homomorphism. The reader should verify the assertions (2.5) and (2.6).

2.5 If f_1 and f_2 are $\mathbb{Z}G$-linear, then $N(f_2ff_1) = f_2N(f)f_1$. □

2.6 If B is a free (or projective) $\mathbb{Z}G$-module, then each $\mathbb{Z}G$-linear homomorphism $h : B \to C$ has the form $N(f)$ for some $\mathbb{Z}$-linear $f : B \to C$. □

Choose $f : F \to F$ such that $N(f) = \mathrm{id}$.
Given $h : F \to \mathbb{Z} \in \mathrm{Hom}_{\mathbb{Z}G}(F,\mathbb{Z})$, then $|G|hfi=N(hfi)=hN(f)i=hi$, so that the image of i^* is contained in $\{k|G|\mathrm{id} \mid k\in\mathbb{Z}\}$. By hypothesis, there exists $f : F \to \mathbb{Z}$ such that $fi = \mathrm{id}$. Then $|G|\mathrm{id} = N(fi) = N(f)i \in \text{image } i^*$. □

In the sense of homological algebra we have $H^n(G;\mathbb{Z}) \cong \mathrm{Ext}^n_{\mathbb{Z}G}(\mathbb{Z},\mathbb{Z})$ and elements in the latter group are represented by n-fold extensions

$$0 \to \mathbb{Z} \to A_{n-1} \to \dots \to A_0 \to \mathbb{Z} .$$

As an exercise the reader may show: The extension (2.1) can be taken as a generator of $H^n(G;\mathbb{Z})$. See MACLANE [1963], III, 5 and 6 for back ground.

2.7 Example. Let $G = \{1,t,t^2,\dots,t^{m-1}\}$ be the cyclic group of order m with generator t. The standard action of G on S^1 given by $t : S^1 \to S^1$, $z \mapsto \exp(2\pi i/m)z$ has a G-equivariant triangulation with O-simplices $\exp(2\pi ik/m) = z_k$ for $0 \le k < m$.

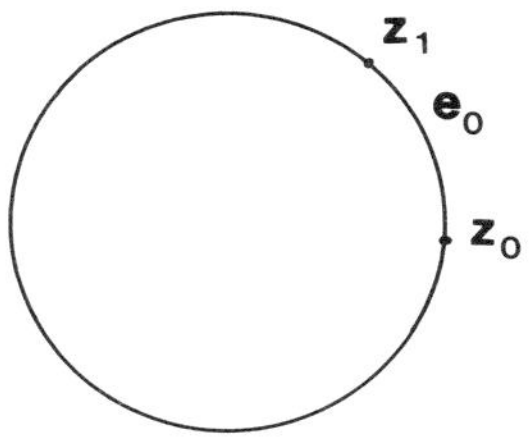

The cellular chain complex leads to an exact sequence

$$0 \to \mathbb{Z} \xrightarrow{i} C_1 \xrightarrow{d} C_0 \xrightarrow{\varepsilon} \mathbb{Z} \to 0,$$

where C_1 and C_0 are free $\mathbb{Z}G$-modules of rank one with basis e_0 and z_0 respectively. This sequence can be identified with

$$0 \to \mathbb{Z} \xrightarrow{i} \mathbb{Z}G \xrightarrow{d} \mathbb{Z}G \xrightarrow{\varepsilon} \mathbb{Z} \to 0$$

$\varepsilon(\sum n_g g) = \sum n_g$, $i(1) = 1 + t + \dots + t^{m-1} =: N$, d multiplication by $t-1$. (This uses $de_0 = z_1 - z_0 = tz_0 - z_0$.) From this sequence we obtain, via splicing, the standard periodic resolution

$$0 \leftarrow \mathbb{Z} \xleftarrow{\varepsilon} \mathbb{Z}G \xleftarrow{t-1} \mathbb{Z}G \xleftarrow{N} \mathbb{Z}G \xleftarrow{t-1} \mathbb{Z}G \xleftarrow{N} \mathbb{Z}G \dots$$

We now describe a more geometric derivation of the previous results. Let $EG \to BG$ be the universal G-principal bundle of G (see e.g. TOM DIECK [1987], I.8). Let X be a homotopy representation of G with free action of dimension $n-1$. The fibre bundle $p: EG\times_G X \to BG$ is a spherical bundle. Suppose again that G acts trivially on $H^{n-1}(X;\mathbb{Z})$. Then this spherical bundle is orientable and has a Gysin sequence (see SPANIER [1966], p. 260)

$$\ldots \to H^k(BG) \xrightarrow{e(X)} H^{k+n}(BG) \xrightarrow{p^*} H^{k+n}(EG\times_G X) \to \ldots$$

The map $e(X)$ is given by multiplication with the Euler class $e(X) \in H^n(BG)$ of the sphere bundle. The definition of $e(X)$ requires an orientation of the sphere bundle. This can be specified by a generator of $H^{n-1}(X)$. The projection $EG\times_G X \to X/G$ is a fibration with contractible fibre EG and therefore a homotopy equivalence (see DOLD [1963]). Since X/G is $(n-1)$-dimensional we have $H^k(EG\times_G X) = 0$ for $k \geq n$.
Thus we see that multiplication by $e(X)$ induces an isomorphism $H^k(BG) \cong H^{k+n}(BG)$ for $k>0$. The cohomology groups $H^k(BG;\mathbb{Z})$ are isomorphic to $H^k(G;\mathbb{Z})$, see MacLANE [1963], IV.11.5. Thus we see again that G must have periodic cohomology, and moreover, $e(X)$ is a periodicity generator.

The following basic result has been obtained by SWAN [1960].

2.8 Theorem. Let $e \in H^n(BG)$ be a periodicity generator (i.e. multiplication by e induces isomorphisms $H^k(BG) \to H^{k+n}(BG)$ for $k>0$). Then there exists an $(n-1)$-dimensional G-complex X with free G-action and trivial G-action on $H^{n-1}(X)$ such that $e(X) = e$. The oriented G-homotopy type of X is uniquely determined by e. □

For an algebraic analysis of groups with periodic cohomology see CARTAN - EILENBERG [1956], XII.11. Let us mention the following results.

2.9 Theorem. The following assertions about G are equivalent:
(i) G has periodic cohomology of period $n>0$.
(ii) $H^n(G;\mathbb{Z}) \cong \mathbb{Z}/|G|$.
(iii) $H^n(G;\mathbb{Z})$ contains an element of order $|G|$.
Moreover, each element of order $|G|$ is a periodicity generator. □

2.10 Theorem. The following assertions about G are equivalent:

(i) G has periodic cohomology.

(ii) Every abelian subgroup of G is cyclic.

(iii) Every p-subgroup of G is either cyclic or a generalized quaternion group.

(iv) Every Sylow subgroup of G is either cyclic or a generalized quaternion group. □

A generalized quaternion group of order 4m is given by generators and relations as follows

$$Q_{4m} = \langle A,B \mid A^m = B^2,\ BAB^{-1} = A^{-1} \rangle .$$

The group Q_{4m} may be regarded as a subgroup of the group of quaternions of norm 1 by setting

$$A \mapsto \exp(\pi i/m),\ B \mapsto j.$$

The element A generates a cyclic normal subgroup of index 2.

In the terminology introduced after (1.6) we can restate (2.10) as follows: A group G has periodic cohomology if and only if it satisfies all p^2-conditions.

Theorem (2.10) is the starting point for a classification of groups with periodic cohomology. For solvable groups see WOLF [1967], Chapter 6. By way of example we describe some of the groups.

2.11 Theorem. (i) Let G be a group of order N such that every Sylow subgroup is cyclic. Then G is generated by two elements A and B with defining relations

$$A^m = 1 = B^n\ ,\ BAB^{-1} = A^r$$

with

$$N = mn,\ ((r-1)n,m) = 1,\ r^n \equiv 1 \bmod m.$$

The commutator group $[G,G]$ is generated by A. Any group given by the relations above has order N and has every Sylow subgroup cyclic.
(ii) Let d be the order of r in $\mathbb{Z}/m^*$, the units of the ring $\mathbb{Z}/m$. Then $d|n$ and G satisfies all pq-conditions if and only if (p prime, $p|d \Rightarrow p|\frac{n}{d}$).

<u>Proof.</u> WOLF [1967], Theorem 5.4.1. □

The simplest type of group which does not satisfy all pq-conditions is thus the following. Let p and q be primes. Suppose $q|p-1$. Let $r^q \equiv 1 \bmod p$, $r \not\equiv 1$.
Then

2.12 $$G_{p,q} = \langle A,B \mid A^p = 1 = B^q,\ BAB^{-1} = A^r \rangle .$$

Special cases are the dihedral groups D_{2p} considered earlier. This group has (minimal) period $2p$

Let us call the G-complexes provided by (2.8) <u>Swan complexes</u>. It should be noted that the Swan complexes cannot always be chosen as finite complexes. This fact is the origin of the theory of finiteness obstructions for CW-complexes.

Let X and Y be homotopy representations with free G-action and trivial G-action on cohomology. Then the join $X*Y$ is again a homotopy representation of the same type. We call X oriented if we have specified a generator (= an orientation) of $H^{n-1}(X)$, $\mathrm{Dim}(X) = n$. If X and Y are oriented then $X*Y$ inherits an orientation such that $e(X*Y) = e(X)e(Y)$ holds. We call X and X' oriented G-homotopy equivalent if there exists a G-homotopy equivalence $f : X \to X'$ mapping orientation class to orientation class; we then have $e(X) = e(X')$. Let $V^{\infty}(G;\text{ free})$ denote the Grothendieck group of oriented G-homotopy representations with free action and trivial action on cohomology (with respect to oriented G-homotopy equivalence and join as composition law).

Given a group G with periodic cohomology one can localize $H^*(BG)$ with respect to the periodicity generators. The result is the Tate-cohomology ring $\hat{H}^*(BG)$ of G (see CARTAN - EILENBERG [1956]). Let

$$\mathrm{Per}\ \hat{H}^*(BG)$$

denote the multiplicative group of periodicity generators of $\hat{H}^*(BG)$.

<u>2.13 Example</u>. Let $G = \mathbb{Z}/m$. Then

$$\tilde{H}^*(BG) \cong x \cdot \mathbb{Z}/m[x]$$

with $x = e(V_1) \in H^2(BG)$, V_1 the standard representation (1.1). One has $e(V_1) = kx$ and therefore

$$e\Big(\sum_{(k,m)=1} n(k)V_k\Big) = \prod_{(k,m)=1} (kx)^{n(k)} .$$

Localization with respect to periodicity generators yields

$$\hat{H}^*(BG) \cong \mathbb{Z}/m\,[x,x^{-1}]$$

(an isomorphism of graded rings).

The result (2.8) of SWAN implies directly

<u>2.14 Theorem</u>. The assignment $X \mapsto e(X)$ induces an isomorphism

$$V^\infty(G;\ \mathrm{free}) \cong \mathrm{Per}\ \hat{H}^*(BG). \quad \square$$

We have an exact sequence

$$0 \to \mathbb{Z}/|G|^* \to V^\infty(G;\ \mathrm{free}) \xrightarrow{d} \mathbb{Z} \to 0,$$

where d maps X to $q^{-1}\,\mathrm{Dim}\,X(1)$ if $q > 0$ denotes the minimal period.

Suppose

$$0 \to \mathbb{Z} \to C_{n-1} \to C_{n-2} \to \dots \to C_0 \to \mathbb{Z} \to 0$$

$$0 \to \mathbb{Z} \to D_{n-1} \to D_{n-2} \to \dots \to D_0 \to \mathbb{Z} \to 0$$

are two periodic resolutions for G with C_i and D_i projective $\mathbb{Z}G$-modules. By the standard comparison lemma for projective resolutions of homological algebra there exists a commutative diagram

2.15
$$\begin{array}{ccccccccc} \mathbb{Z} & \xrightarrow{i} & C_{n-1} & \to & \dots & \to & C_0 & \to & \mathbb{Z} \\ \downarrow f & & \downarrow f_{n-1} & & & & \downarrow f_0 & & \downarrow id \\ \mathbb{Z} & \to & D_{n-1} & \to & \dots & \to & D_0 & \to & \mathbb{Z} \end{array} .$$

If $f(1) = d$ we call d the degree $d(f)$ of f. If C_* and D_* are the cellular chain complexes of Swan complexes X and Y and if $h : X \to Y$ is a cellular G-map, then f and f_i are induced by h and d is the degree $d(h)$ of h in the sense of algebraic topology.

2.16 Lemma. Let f' and f_i' be another set of $\mathbb{Z}G$-homomorphisms making (2.15) commutative. Then $d(f) \equiv d(f') \bmod |G|$.

Proof. Two chain maps between resolutions are chain homotopic (MacLANE [1963], III.6.1). In our case this implies $f - f' = ki$ for some $k : C_{n-1} \to \mathbb{Z}$. Now apply (2.4). □

Thus the degree of $h : X \to Y$ depends modulo $|G|$ only on X and Y and is independ of the map h.
The next proposition makes this dependence more explicit.

2.17 Proposition. $h^*e(Y) = d(h)e(X)$.

2.18 Corollary. $d(h)$ is prime to $|G|$. □

A proof of (2.17) follows by identifying (2.1) with a generator of $H^n(G) \cong H^n(BG)$ and then using the proof of (2.3).

3. Tangential structures on Swan complexes.

Let G be a finite group and P a subgroup of G. A G-representation V is called P-free if the restriction $res_P V$ is a free P-representation. Let $G(p)$ denote a p-Sylow subgroup of G.

3.1 Lemma. Suppose G possesses a $G(p)$-free representation for each prime p. Then G has periodic cohomology.

Proof. (2.2) and (2.10). □

Let $H(1),\ldots,H(r)$ be subgroups of G such that the orders $|H(i)|$ and $|H(j)|$ for $i \neq j$ are relatively prime and such that $|G| = \prod_i |H(i)|$. Suppose G possesses an $H(i)$-free representation V_i for each i. Then again G must have periodic cohomology. We assume given an $H(i)$-free complex representation V_i for each i such that $n = \dim_{\mathbb{R}} V_i$ is independent of i. The unit sphere SV_i in V_i is canonically oriented. We let $a_i G \times_{H(i)} SV_i$ be the disjoint union of $|a_i|$ copies of the G-manifold $G \times_{H(i)} SV_i$, with opposite orientation if $a_i<0$. The G-manifold

$$3.2 \qquad \coprod_{i=1}^{r} a_i G \times_{H(i)} SV_i = M = M(a_1,\ldots,a_r)$$

carries a free G-action.

3.3 Assumption. n is a period of G. (This can actually be proved. See SWAN [1960a] for the determination of the period.)

Let X be an $(n-1)$-dimensional Swan complex for G. We assume that X is oriented, i.e. a generator for $H^{n-1}(X;\mathbb{Z}) \cong \mathbb{Z}$ is chosen, and G acts trivially on cohomology. Then it makes sense to talk about the degree of a map $f : S^{n-1} \to X$.

3.4 Proposition. Suppose there exists an $H(i)$-map $f_i : SV_i \to \operatorname{res}_{H(i)} X$ of degree one for each i. Then the integers $a_1, \ldots, a_r$ can be chosen such that there exists a tangential G-map (1.10)

$$\begin{array}{ccc} T(M) & \xrightarrow{\quad F \quad} & X \times U \\ \downarrow & & \downarrow \\ M & \xrightarrow{\quad f \quad} & X \end{array} \tag{3.5}$$

with f of degree one. Here U is a suitable G-representation and $T(M) = T(M) \oplus k\varepsilon$ is the stable tangent bundle of M.

Proof. In general, an H-map $f : Y \to X$ yields a G-map $f' : G \times_H Y \to X$, $(g,y) \mapsto gf(y)$. We apply this construction to the maps f_i of degree one and obtain a G-map

$$f : M(a_1, \ldots, a_r) \to X$$

of degree

$$\sum_{i=1}^{r} a_i \,|G/H(i)|. \tag{3.6}$$

By our assumption about the orders of the $H(i)$ we have $(|G/H(1)|, \ldots, |G/H(r)|) = 1$. Hence we can find integers a_i such that the sum (3.6) equals one.

Thus it remains to be shown that the resulting map f can be covered by a bundle map F. We have the following bundle isomorphisms

$$T(G \times_H SV) \oplus \varepsilon \cong$$

$$G \times_H (TSV \oplus \varepsilon) \cong$$

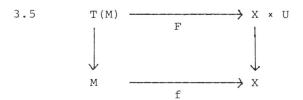

$$G\times_H(SV \times V) \cong$$
$$(G\times_H SV) \times V$$

for $H = H(i)$ and $V = V_i$. We have used the fact that the H-bundle $TSV \oplus \varepsilon$ is canonically isomorphic to the product bundle $SV \times V$. Also note that there is a canonical homeomorphism

$$G\times_H(A \times B) \to (G\times_H A) \times B, \ (g,a,b) \mapsto (g,a,gb)$$

of G-spaces, if B is a G-space.

Thus it suffices to find a G-representation U such that each $SV_i \times (V_i \oplus \mathbb{R}^k)$ admits an $H(i)$-bundle map

$$F_i : SV_i \times (V_i \times \mathbb{R}^k) \to U.$$

The existence of F_i will be shown in two steps.

Let $K_H(Y)$ be the Grothendieck ring of complex H-vector bundles over the H-space Y (H-equivariant K-theory). For basic properties of equivariant K-theory see ATIYAH [1967], [1968], SEGAL [1968]. Associating to an H-representation U the trivial bundle $Y \times U \to Y$ provides us with a homomorphism

$$\alpha : R(H) \to K_H(Y).$$

We denote the image of $U_1 - U_2 \in R(H)$ under α with the same symbols.

<u>3.7 Lemma</u>. There exists $x \in R(G)$ such that for each i the $H(i)$-restriction maps x to $V_i - n \in K_{H(i)}(SV_i)$.

<u>Proof</u>. Since SV_i is a free $H(i)$-space we obtain an isomorphism

$$K_{H(i)}(SV_i) \cong K(SV_i/H(i))$$

by passing to orbit spaces. The element $V_i - n$ lies in the reduced group $\widetilde{K}(SV_i/H(i))$. The Atiyah - Hirzebruch spectral sequence (WHITEHEAD [1978], XIII.6) with E_2-term $\widetilde{H}^p(SV_i/H(i);K^{-p})$ shows that $\widetilde{K}(SV_i/H(i))$ is a finite group which is annihilated by a power of $|H(i)|$. Since the V_i are G-representations the torsion elements $x_i = V_i - n$ are in the image of the restriction $R(G) \to K_{H(i)}(SV_i)$. Since the $|H(i)|$ are relatively prime we can find (Chinese remainder theorem) an element x which maps to x_i for each i. □

We write the x of (3.7) as a difference $V - W$ of genuine representations V and W. We deduce the existence of $H(i)$-maps

$$SV_i \times (V_i \oplus W) \to V \oplus \mathbb{R}^n$$

(with possibly different V and W).

<u>3.8 Lemma</u>. There exists a G-representation W^- such that the G-bundle $X \times (W \oplus W^-)$ is isomorphic to a bundle $a\varepsilon$.

<u>Proof</u>. As in the proof of (3.7) we use the fact that $\widetilde{K}_G(X) \cong \widetilde{K}(X/G)$ is a finite group annihilated by some power of $|G|$. This means that some multiple $a(X\times_G W)$ is a stably trivial bundle. Translating this statement back to X shows that W^- can be chosen to be of the form $bW \oplus c\varepsilon$. □

<u>3.9 Corollary</u>. The $H(i)$-bundles $SV_i \times (W \oplus W^-)$ are trivial, say isomorphic to $k\varepsilon$. Thus there exist $H(i)$-maps

$$F_i : SV_i \times (V_i \oplus \mathbb{R}^k) \to V \oplus W^- \oplus \mathbb{R}^n =: U. \quad \square$$

This finishes the proof of (3.4). We now describe some examples where $H(i)$-free representations can easily be found.

<u>3.10 The groups</u> $G_{m,n}$.

Let $G = G_{m,n}$ be the group provided by (2.11) for odd m and n. Let $H = \langle A \rangle$ and $K = \langle B \rangle$ be the subgroups generated by A and B respectively. If d is the order of $r \in \mathbb{Z}/m^*$, then the conjugation action of K on H has kernel L of order n/d. We have a semi-direct product sequence

$$1 \to H \to G_{m,n} \to K \to 1.$$

Let $D \triangleleft G_{m,n}$ be the normal subgroup which is the pre-image of $L \subset K$. Note that D is cyclic and d is odd.

The complex irreducible representations V of G which are H-free are obtained as follows (see SERRE [1971], 8.2). Let η be a one-dimensional D-representation which is H-free. Then the induced representation $\mathrm{Ind}_D^G \eta$ is H-free too. There exists η such that $V \cong \mathrm{Ind}_D^G \eta$.

A faithful K-representation can be lifted to G and yields a K-free representation.

The group G has period $2d$. There exist H-free and K-free representations V_H and V_K of complex dimension dk, $k \geq 1$. We thus can apply (3.4) if we can find maps $f_H : SV_H \to X$ and $f_K : SV_K \to X$ of degree one; in other words: The G-homotopy type of X must satisfy

$$\mathrm{res}_H X \simeq SV_H \quad \text{and} \quad \mathrm{res}_K X \simeq SV_K.$$

The homotopy type of X is determined by its Euler-class $e(X) \in H^{2dk}(G;\mathbb{Z})$, see (2.8).

The restrictions to H and K induce an isomorphism:

$$\begin{array}{ccc} H^{2dk}(G;\mathbb{Z}) & \xrightarrow{\cong} & H^{2dk}(H;\mathbb{Z}) \times H^{2dk}(K;\mathbb{Z}). \\ \| \wr & & \| \wr \\ \mathbb{Z}/|G| & & \mathbb{Z}/m \times \mathbb{Z}/n \end{array}$$

We can find V_K such that $e(V_K)$ is any given element of $\mathbb{Z}/n^*$. Let η be the standard representation of $H = \langle A \rangle$ given by $A : \mathbb{C} \to \mathbb{C}$, $z \mapsto \exp(2\pi i/m)z$. Let a be prime to m, extend η^a to a D-representation and let $V(a) = \mathrm{Ind}_D^G \eta^a$. Then $\mathrm{res}_H V(a)$ is the direct sum of the K-conjugates of η^a. Let the isomorphism $H^{2t}(H;\mathbb{Z}) \cong \mathbb{Z}/m$ be chosen such that $e(\eta)^t \mapsto 1$. Then, computing modulo m and using that d is odd,

$$e(\mathrm{res}_H V(a)) = a(ra)\ (r^2 a)\ldots(r^{d-1}a)$$
$$= a^d r^{d(d-1)/2} = a^d.$$

We conclude that we can realize the d-th powers in $\mathrm{Per}H^{2dk}(H;\mathbb{Z}) = \mathbb{Z}/m^*$.

At this point we should note that in order to find a compact manifold which is G-homotopy equivalent to X we must know that X has the G-homotopy type of a finite complex. It is a difficult problem to determine exactly which elements $e \in H^{2dk}(G;\mathbb{Z})$ are Euler classes of finite Swan complexes. But in the case at hand we are lucky since the following holds true.

<u>3.11 Proposition</u>. Suppose $x \in H^{2dk}(G_{m,n})$ is a periodicity generator which restricts to a d-th power in $\mathrm{Per}H^{2dk}(H;\mathbb{Z}) = \mathbb{Z}/m^*$ under the isomorphism described above. Then x is the Euler class of a finite Swan complex.

<u>Proof</u>. See WALL [1979]. □

We can now apply the general results of surgery theory, in particular the fact that the groups $L_n^h(\mathbb{Z}G)$ for n odd and $|G|$ odd are zero, to obtain from (3.4) and (3.11):

<u>3.12 Proposition</u>. Let $|G_{m,n}|$ be odd. Let $x \in H^{2dk}(G_{m,n})$ be a periodicity generator which restricts to a d-th power in $\mathrm{Per}H^{2dk}(H)$. Then there exists a smooth space form X with Euler class $e(X) = x$. □

The first examples of smooth space forms for $G_{p,q}$ were found by PETRIE [1971]. For the method of proof used here see PETRIE [1979].

3.13 The groups $Q(8a,b,c)$.
Let a,b,c be odd natural numbers which are pairwise relatively prime. Let A,B,C be cyclic groups of order a,b,c. Let $Q(8) = \langle x,y \mid x^2 = y^2, \quad yxy^{-1} = x^{-1} \rangle$ be the quaternion group of order 8. The group $Q = Q(8a,b,c)$ is defined by the semi-direct product

$$1 \to A \times B \times C \to Q \to Q(8) \to 1$$

where the action of $Q(8)$ on $A \times B \times C$ is given as follows:

x inverts $B \times C$, zentralizes A
y inverts $A \times C$, zentralizes B
$xy = z$ inverts $A \times B$, zentralizes C.

This group has period 4.

There exists a faithful 2-dimensional complex representation V_Q of $Q(8)$ (see text after (2.10)) which lifts to a $Q(8)$-free representation of Q.

Let η_A be a faithful one-dimensional representation of A. Lift this to a representation of $A \times B \times C$ with trivial action of $B \times C$. Conjugation by x does not change η_A. Therefore, η_A can be extended to the subgroup X generated by $A \times B \times C$ and x, with trivial action of x. Let $V(\eta_A) = \mathrm{Ind}_X^Q \eta_A$. This is a two-dimensional A-free representation. In a similar manner we can find B-free and C-free representations.

Again one has to determine the homotopy types X which satisfy

$$\mathrm{res}_D X \simeq SV(\eta_D) \qquad \text{for } D = A,B,C$$
$$\mathrm{res}_{Q(8)} X \simeq SV_Q$$

and find the finite ones among them. This is not easy and will not be discussed here.

4. The Picard group of the Burnside ring.

A basic invariant of the G-homotopy type of a homotopy representation for G is its dimension function. In this section we deal with the homotopy classification of homotopy representations with the same dimension function.

Let X and Y be G-homotopy representations with $\operatorname{Dim}X = \operatorname{Dim}Y$. We consider G-maps $f : X \to Y$. For each subgroup H of G the H-fixed point mapping $f^H : X^H \to Y^H$ has a degree, provided we have oriented the spaces X^H and Y^H. In order to simplify the discussion of orientations, we consider only orientable homotopy representations. Let NH denote the normalizer of H in G. Then X^H inherits an NH-action from the G-action on X. The homotopy representation X is called <u>orientable</u> if for all $H \subset G$ the NH-action on $\tilde{H}^{n(H)-1}(X^H;\mathbb{Z})$ is trivial (recall $n(H)-1 = \dim X^H$). An <u>orientation</u> of X is a choice of a generator

$$z(H) \in \tilde{H}^{n(H)-1}(X^H;\mathbb{Z})$$

for each subgroup H such that $X^H \neq \emptyset$. An orientation is called <u>coherent</u> if it has the following properties:

(i) Let $H \subset K$, $n(H) = n(K)$ and let $i : X^K \subset X^H$ be the inclusion. Then $i^*z(H) = z(K)$.

(ii) Let $gHg^{-1} = K$ and let $l_g : X^H \to X^K$ be the left translation by g. Then $l_g^*z(K) = z(H)$.

It is not difficult to show (see TOM DIECK [1987], II.10)

<u>4.1 Lemma</u>. Suppose X is orientable. Then X possesses a coherent orientation. □

From now on we assume that homotopy representations are orientable and coherently oriented. If $f : X \to Y$ is a G-map between two such homotopy representations, then

$$d(f) : H \mapsto \text{degree } f^H = d(f^H)$$

is called the <u>degree function</u> of f. If H and K are conjugate subgroups, then f^H and f^K have the same degree. Therefore, we consider $d(f)$ as a function on conjugacy classes of subgroups:

4.2 $\qquad d(f) \in C(G)$.

(In order to have $d(f)$ defined for all subgroups we let $d(f)(H) = 1$ in case $X^H = \emptyset$.)

The degree function is a stable invariant: If Z is another homotopy representation then f and $f*id(Z)$ have the same degree function. ($X * Z$ inherits a canonical orientation from X and Z.)

We refer to TOM DIECK [1987], II.10 for a proof of the following result.

<u>4.2 Proposition.</u> Let X and Y be homotopy representations with the same dimension function. Let c be a multiple of $|G|$.

(i) There exists a G-map $f : X \to Y$ with degrees prime to c.

(ii) Suppose $f : X \to Y$ has degrees prime to c. There exists a G-map $h : Y \to X$ such that for all $H \subset G$

$$d(f^H)d(h^H) \equiv 1 \mod c.$$

(iii) The set of all stable degree functions $X * Z \to X * Z$ is a subring $A(G) \subset C(G)$ which is independent of X.

(iv) $|G|C(G) \subset A(G)$. □

Since $|G|C(G) \subset A(G)$, we can consider the following rings

$$\bar{C} = \bar{C}(G) = C(G)/|G|C(G) \supset \bar{A} = \bar{A}(G) = A(G)/|G|C(G).$$

Let S^* denote the group of units of a ring S. Consider the multiplicative group

4.3 $\qquad \mathrm{Pic}(G) := \bar{C}^*/C^*\bar{A}^*$.

Given $x = X - Y \in v^\infty(G)$ one can always find representing homotopy representations X and Y which are orientable.

Choose coherent orientations and let $f : X \to Y$ be a G-map with degrees prime to $|G|$. Then the degree function $d(f)$ represents an element $[d(f)] \in \mathrm{Pic}(G)$. A different choice of orientations does not change $[d(f)]$, since we have divided by the group C^* of all sign-functions. Suppose $x = X - Y = X' - Y'$ and $f : X \to Y$ and $f' : X' \to Y'$ are maps with degrees prime to c. One can show $[d(f)] = [d(f')]$. Therefore, we have a well defined map

4.4 $\qquad D : V^{\infty}(G) \to \mathrm{Pic}(G), \quad x \mapsto [d(f)]$

which is obviously a homomorphism.

<u>4.5 Theorem</u>. The map D is an isomorphism.

<u>Proof</u>. TOM DIECK - PETRIE [1978]; TOM DIECK [1987], II.10. □

<u>Remark</u>. The ring $A(G)$ is the <u>Burnside ring</u> of G. See TOM DIECK [1987] for various definitions and properties of this ring. The group $\mathrm{Pic}(G)$ can be interpreted as the Picard group of $A(G)$: The group of isomorphism classes of projective $A(G)$-modules of rank one with tensor product as composition law; see TOM DIECK [1985] for properties and computations.

The injectivity of the map D has the following interpretation: Given Y. The stable homotopy type of a homotopy representation X with $\mathrm{Dim}X = \mathrm{Dim}Y$ is determined by chosing a G-map $f : X \to Y$ with degrees prime to $|G|$ (= with <u>invertible degree function</u>) and looking at $d(f) \in \mathrm{Pic}(G)$.

<u>Remark</u>. One can also define Picard groups which detect the unstable homotopy type; see LAITINEN [1986].

For abelian groups G one can give a fairly explicit description of $\mathrm{Pic}(G)$. It is actually simplex to describe the "orientable" version

4.6 $\qquad \mathrm{Inv}(G) := \bar{C}^*/\bar{A}^*.$

Let G be abelian and let μ denote the <u>Möbius function</u> of the subgroup lattice. This is a function $\mu : \Phi(G) \to \mathbb{Z}$ from subgroups to $\mathbb{Z}$ defined by the properties

4.7
$$\mu(1) = 1$$
$$\sum_{K \subset H} \mu(K) = 0 \qquad \text{for } H \neq 1.$$

If G is cyclic, then $\mu(H) = \mu'(|H|)$, where μ' denotes the Möbius function from elementary number theory. If G is a p-group, then $\mu(H) \neq 0$ if and only if H is an elementary abelian group (i.e. $H = (\mathbb{Z}/p)^d$ for some d) and

4.8
$$\mu(H) = (-1)^d p^{d(d-1)/2}, \qquad |H| = p^d.$$

Let $d(H) : \bar{C}(G)^* \to \mathbb{Z}/|G|^*$ be evaluation at H. Define

4.9
$$n'(H) : \bar{C}(G)^* \to \mathbb{Z}/|G/H|^*$$

by
$$n(H) = \prod_{K \supset H} d(K)^{\mu(K/H)}.$$

(We also apply reduction $\mathbb{Z}/|G| \to \mathbb{Z}/|G/H|$.)

4.10 Theorem. The homomorphisms $n'(H)$ factor over the quotient $\bar{C}(G)^* \to \mathrm{Inv}(G)$ and induce $n(H) : \mathrm{Inv}(G) \to \mathbb{Z}/|G/H|^*$. The product

$$(n(H) \mid H \subset G) : \mathrm{Inv}(G) \to \prod_{H \subset G} \mathbb{Z}/|G/H|^*$$

is an isomorphism.

Proof. TOM DIECK [1978], [1985]. □

4.11 Example. Let $G = \mathbb{Z}/p \times \mathbb{Z}/p$. The group G has $p+1$ subgroup $H_0, \ldots, H_p$ of order p. Therefore, one has maps

$$n(1) : \mathrm{Inv}(G) \to \mathbb{Z}/p^{2*}, \quad d \mapsto d(1)d(G)^p \prod_{i=0}^{p} d(H_i)^{-1}$$

$$n(H_i) : \mathrm{Inv}(G) \to \mathbb{Z}/p^{*}, \quad d \mapsto d(H_i)d(G)^{-1}.$$

In geometrical terms this means: Let $f : X \to Y$ be a G-map with invertible degree function $d(f)$. Then

$$n(f) = d(f)d(f^G)^p \prod_{i=0}^{p} d(f^{H_i})^{-1} \mod p^2$$

is independent of f and depends only on the G-homotopy type of X and Y. Similarly for $n(f^{H_i}) = d(f^{H_i})d(f^G)^{-1} \mod p$.

Let $f : S(V_k) \to S(V_1)$, $z \mapsto z^t$, with $kt \equiv 1 \mod p$, be a G-map between representations of $G/H_i \cong \mathbb{Z}/p$ (notation (1.1)). Then $d(f) = t = d(f^{H_i})$ and $d(f^H) = 1$ for $H \neq 1, H_i$. Therefore, only $n(H_i)$ yields a non-trivial value. Since representations are direct sums of one-dimensional representations we conclude that under the isomorphism (4.10) maps between representations yield the subgroup

$$\prod_{H \subset G} \mathbb{Z}/|G/H|^*, \quad |G/H| \text{ cyclic.}$$

A similar statement holds true for abelian groups in general. Thus if $n(1) \not\equiv 1 \mod p^2$, then a non-linear homotopy type must be involved.

Suppose p is odd. It follows easily from the Borel-relation for dimension functions (see TOM DIECK [1987], III.5) that every homotopy representation X of $\mathbb{Z}/p \times \mathbb{Z}/p$ has the dimension function of a representation $S(V)$. Choose a map $f : X \to S(V)$ with invertible degree function. Then it can be shown that X has the G-homotopy type of a finite complex if and only if $n(1)$ is a p-th power $\mod p^2$. Therefore, there exist finite non-linear homotopy representations. They also exist as smooth representations forms, see TOM DIECK - LÖFFLER [1985].

Let X be a homotopy representation of the abelian p-group G, p odd. Let SV be a representation sphere with $\operatorname{Dim}X = \operatorname{Dim}SV$ (see (5.5)). Let $\omega(X, SV) \in \operatorname{Inv}(G)$ denote the element represented by an invertible degree function. Then the following holds.

4.11 Theorem. X has the G-homotopy type of a finite complex if and only if for every $H \subset G$ such that G/H is non-cyclic the element $n(H)$ is a p^{t-1}-th power mod $p^t = |G/H|$.

Proof. TOM DIECK [1985].

5. Cyclic groups.

5.1 Theorem. Let $G = \mathbb{Z}/m$ be cyclic. Then the canonical homomorphisms

$$JO(G) \to V(G) \to V^{\infty}(G)$$

are isomorphisms.

Proof. We first show that $JO(G)$ and $V^{\infty}(G)$ have the same group of dimension functions. Let V be a representation of $G = \mathbb{Z}/m$. Write

$$V = \bigoplus_{d \mid m} V(d)$$

where $V(d)$ contains the irreducible summands with kernel $\mathbb{Z}/d$. The dimension function n of SV satisfies $n(\mathbb{Z}/k) = \sum_{k \mid d} \dim V(d)$. Using Möbius inversion from elementary number theory ($F(n) = \sum_{d \mid m} f(d) \iff f(n) = \sum_{d \mid m} \mu(d) F(d)$) we obtain

5.2 $$\dim V(k) = \sum_{d \mid \frac{m}{k}} \mu(d) n(\mathbb{Z}/kd).$$

An irreducible real representation of $\mathbb{Z}/m$ is two-dimensional if $|m/k| > 2$ and one-dimensional otherwise. We obtain:

5.3 Lemma. A function $n \in C(G)$ is contained in the image of $\mathrm{Dim} : JO(G) \to C(G)$ if and only if

5.4 $$\sum_{d \mid \frac{m}{k}} \mu(d) n(\mathbb{Z}/kd) \equiv 0 \mod 2$$

whenever $|m/k| > 2$.

Proof of the Lemma. By (5.2) and the remarks thereafter the congruences are necessary. Suppose they are satisfied. Choose representations $V(k)$ and $V'(k)$ with kernel $\mathbb{Z}/k$ such that

$\dim V(k) - \dim V'(k) = \sum \mu(d) n(\mathbb{Z}/kd)$.
Then $\bigoplus_{k|m} V(k) - \bigoplus_{k|m} V'(k) \in RO(G)$ has dimension function n. □

We now show that the dimension function n of every homotopy representation satisfies (5.4). It suffices to consider the case $k = 1$ (otherwise look at the $H=\mathbb{Z}/k$- fixed points as a homotopy representation for G/H). Write $n(k) = n(\mathbb{Z}/k)$. If $|m| > 2$ is a prime power p^t, then the assertion is $n(1) - n(p) \equiv 0$ mod 2. This congruence is one of the basic facts of P.A. Smith theory (see TOM DIECK [1987], III (4.23), (4.31)). If m is not a prime power, then the asserted congruence is a formal consequence of the prime power congruence: If m contains two primes p and q, then $n(1) - n(p) - n(q) + n(pq) \equiv 0$ mod 2, because $n(1) \equiv n(p)$ mod 2 and $n(q) \equiv n(pq)$ mod 2 if p is odd. The general case follows similarly. Actually much more is true. Namely one can show (see TOM DIECK [1987], III (5.4)):

<u>5.5 Theorem.</u> Let G be a finite nilpotent group. Then $\mathrm{Dim} : JO(G) \to C(G)$ and $\mathrm{Dim} : V^{\infty}(G) \to C(G)$ have the same image. □

In order to finish the proof of (5.1) one has to show that the canonical map $jO(G) \to V^{\infty}(G)$ is an isomorphism. This needs some preparation. We begin by computing $jO(G)$ for an abelian group.

Let $G = \mathbb{Z}/m$. Given positive integers $r_1, \dots, r_n$ prime to m, we have the representation $V(r_1, \dots, r_n)$ with free action of $\mathbb{Z}/m \subset S^1$, $\mathbb{Z}/m \times \mathbb{C}^n \to \mathbb{C}^n$, $(\zeta, (z_1, \dots, z_n)) \mapsto (\zeta^{r_1} z_1, \dots, \zeta^{r_n} z_n)$ with unit sphere $SV(r_1, \dots, r_n) =: S(r_i)$. A G-map f between two such spheres is a G-homotopy equivalence if and only if it is an ordinary homotopy equivalence and this is the case if and only if f has degree ± 1 (TOM DIECK [1987], II(2.7)). We orient $S(r_i)$ in a canonical manner using the standard orientation of $\mathbb{C}^n$. The map $f : S^1 \to S^1$, $z \mapsto z^t$ satisfies $f(\zeta^r z) = \zeta^{rt} f(z)$. Therefore, this is an equivariant map $SV(r) \to SV(1)$ whenever $rt \equiv 1$ mod m. The degree of this map is t. Note that $S(r_i) = SV(r_1) * SV(r_2) * \dots * SV(r_n)$.

Choose integers t_i such that $r_i t_i \equiv s_i$ mod m. Applying the join construction to maps like f above we obtain a map $h : S(r_i) \to S(s_i)$ of degree $\prod_{i=1}^{n} t_i$ (using $\deg(f_1 * f_2) = \deg f_1 \cdot \deg f_2$). Now given a map $f : S(r_i) \to S(s_i)$ of degree d we can find another map of degree $d \pm |G|$ as follows: Choose an orientation preserving G-embedding $G \times D^{2n-1} \subset S(r_i)$; pinch the boundary of each disk to a point; assume f is constant on each disk; use the pinching map $S(r_i) \to S(r_i) \vee (G \times S^{2n-1})$ and compose with $f : S(r_i) \to S(s_i)$ and a map of degree ± 1 $S^{2n-1} \to S(s_i)$ extended equivariantly to $G \times S^{2n-1}$.

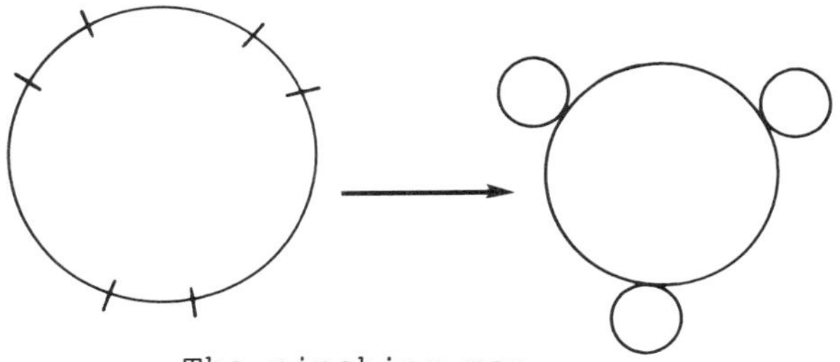

The pinching map

5.6 Proposition. $S(r_i)$ and $S(s_i)$ are G-homotopy equivalent if and only if $r_1 r_2 \cdot \ldots \cdot r_n \equiv \pm s_1 s_2 \cdot \ldots \cdot s_n$ mod m.

Proof. Suppose this congruence is satisfied. If the plus-sign holds we have just shown the existence of an equivariant map of degree one. If the minus-sign holds note that complex conjugation induces a homotopy equivalence $SV(r) \to SV(-r)$ of degree -1.

Suppose $f : S(r_i) \to S(s_i)$ is a G-map. Then we have shown in (2.16) that the degree $d(f)$ modulo m of f is uniquely determined by the oriented spaces $S(r_i)$ and $S(s_i)$. We have shown that there exist maps f satisfying $d(f) r_1 \cdot \ldots \cdot r_n \equiv s_1 \cdot \ldots \cdot s_n$ mod m. Thus if there exists a homotopy equivalence, then the stated congruence must hold. □

Let $jO(G,f)$ be the jO group of G-representations which are direct sums of faithful irreducible representations. Then (5.6) yields the computation

5.7 $\quad jO(G,f) \cong (\mathbb{Z}/m^*)/\{\underline{+}1\}, \quad m = |G|.$

By lifting representations of G/H to G we obtain a homomorphism

5.8 $\quad c_H : jO(G/H,f) \to jO(G).$

5.9 Proposition. $s = (c_H | H \subset G) : \bigoplus_{H \subset G} jO(G/H,f) \to jO(G)$ is an isomorphism.

Proof. Taking H-fixed points defines a map $b_H : jO(G) \to jO(G/H)$. We have $b_H c_K = 0$ if $H \not\subset K$; and for $H \subset K$ this composition equals $jO(G/K,f) \xrightarrow{l} jO(G/K) \xrightarrow{c} jO(G/H)$. Clearly s is surjective. Suppose $\sum c_H x_H = 0$, $x_H \in jO(G/H,f)$. Let K be maximal with $c_K \neq 0$ and apply b_K to this sum. One obtains $c_K l(x_K)$ where $l : jO(G/K,f) \to jO(G/K)$ is the canonical map of type (5.9). Thus it suffices to show that l is injective. This follows from the next proposition. □

5.10 Proposition. Let V and W be free representation of the cyclic group G which are stably homotopy equivalent. Then SV and SW are homotopy equivalent.

Proof. One can use TOM DIECK [1987], II.5, to describe stable maps via congruences between fixed point degrees. □

Let V be a G-representation and $V(H)$ be the sum of the submodules with kernel H. Then (5.9) says that V and W are stably homotopy equivalent if and only if for all $H \subset G$ $V(H)$ and $W(H)$ are stably homotopy equivalent. Using (5.10) one has a similar statement for actual homotopy equivalence.

5.11 Theorem. Let X be a homotopy representation for $G = \mathbb{Z}/m$. Let $\mathrm{Dim}X = \mathrm{Dim}SV$. Suppose that $H \in \mathrm{Iso}\, SV$ implies that V contains an irreducible G-module with kernel H. Then X has linear homotopy type.

Proof. We need to find a representation W such that there exists a G-map $f : X \to SW$ with $\deg f^H = \pm 1$ for all $H \subset G$. Let F be a family of subgroups such that $(H \in F,\ K \supset H \Rightarrow K \in F)$. Suppose we have found U with $\mathrm{Dim} X = \mathrm{Dim} SU$ and $h : X \to SU$ such that $\deg f^H = \pm 1$ for all $H \in F$. Let $K \notin F$ be maximal. If $K \notin \mathrm{Iso}\, SV$, then $\dim V^K = \dim U^H$ for some $K \subset H$, $H \in \mathrm{Iso}\, SV$ and then $X^H \subset X^K$ is a homotopy equivalence (LAITINEN [1986]; TOM DIECK [1987], II.(10.12)). Therefore, $\deg f^K = \pm 1$.
If $K \in \mathrm{Iso}\, SV$, then by our assumption about V, there exist irreducible summands in V with kernel K and, since $\mathrm{Dim}\, SU = \mathrm{Dim}\, SV$, there exist similar summands in U. Let $U(K)$ be the sum of such submodules of U. Then, by changing the summand $U(K)$ of U suitably and thus obtaining U', we can find a G-map $h_1 : SU \to SU'$ such that $\deg h_1^H = 1$ for $H \in F$ and $\deg h_1^K \cdot \deg h^K \equiv 1 \mod |G|$. By the equivariant Hopf theorem (TOM DIECK [1987], II.4) we can find a map $k : X \to SU'$ such that $\deg(k^H) = \pm 1$ for $H \in F \cup \{K\}$. By induction over F we finally arrive at a map $f : X \to SW$ as desired. □

Proof of (5.1). We show that $j : JO(G) \to V^\infty(G)$ is surjective. Let Y be a homotopy representation. By our proof of (5.1) for cyclic G we can find representations V and W such that $\mathrm{Dim}\, X = \mathrm{Dim}\, SV - \mathrm{Dim}\, SW$. Therefore, $Y * SW$ has linear dimension function. By enlarging W if necessary we can assume that $X = Y * SW$ satisfies the hypothesis of (5.11) and therefore has linear homotopy type. This shows that X and hence Y is in the image of j.

We show that j is injective. Suppose that $SV - SW = 0$ in $V^\infty(G)$. This means that there exists a homotopy representation X such that $SV * X$ and $SW * X$ are homotopy equivalent. There exist U_1, U_2 such that $X * SU_1 \simeq SU_2$.
Therefore $SV * SU_2 \simeq SW * SU_2$. □

As a corollary of (5.11) one obtains

<u>5.12 Proposition.</u> Let G be a cyclic p-group. Then a homotopy representation of G has linear homotopy type. □

<u>Remark</u>. For $G = \mathbb{Z}/p \times \mathbb{Z}/q$, $p \neq q$ both odd primes, there exist representation forms with non-linear homotopy type but linear dimension function. It is a consequence of Smith-theory that a representation form for $\mathbb{Z}/p \times \mathbb{Z}/q$ must have linear dimension function. A homotopy representation can have non-linear dimension function.

6. Dihedral goups.

The dihedral goup

$$D_{2m} = \langle A, B \mid A^m = 1 = B^2, \quad BAB^{-1} = A^{-1} \rangle$$

has periodic cohomology of period 4. MILNOR [1957] discovered that D_{2m} cannot act freely on a sphere. We reprove this result and investigate more closely the geometry of representation forms for D_{2m}.

Let D_{2m} act on a space X. Suppose $H = \langle A \rangle$, the subgroup generated by A, has no fixed points. The elements $B(j) := A^j B$, $j = 0, \dots, m-1$, fill up $G \setminus H$ and have order two. If A^{i-j} has no fixed points on X, then the fixed sets $X^{B(i)}$ and $X^{B(j)}$ are disjoint. In particular if A^2 has no fixed points, then $X^B \cap AX^B = X^B \cap X^{B(2)} = \emptyset$.

Let us call a closed manifold X a $\mathbb{Z}/2$-homology k-sphere if $H_*(X;\mathbb{Z}/2) = H_*(S^k;\mathbb{Z}/2)$. If X is a $\mathbb{Z}/2$-homology sphere, then the fixed set of the involution $B(j)$ is again a $\mathbb{Z}/2$-homology sphere by P.A. Smith theory (TOM DIECK [1987], III.4). Suppose that H has no fixed points on the $\mathbb{Z}/2$-homology sphere of dimension $2n-1$, $n \geq 2$. Suppose X^B has dimension $n-1$. Then there is defined a linking number $v \in \mathbb{Z}/2$ of X^B and AX^B (which are disjoint) as follows: Consider the diagram

$$H_{n-1}(X^B) \xrightarrow[i_*]{} H_{n-1}(X \setminus AX^B) \xleftarrow[D]{} H^n(X, AX^B) \xleftarrow[\delta]{} H^{n-1}(AX^B).$$

We use (co-)homology with $\mathbb{Z}/2$-coefficients; the map i is the inclusion, D is Poincaré duality; and δ (from the exact cohomology sequence) is an isomorphism, since the adjacent groups are zero. Since $H_{n-1}(X^B) \cong \mathbb{Z}/2 \cong H^n(AX^B)$ the map i_* either zero ($v = 0$) or an isomorphism ($v = 1$).

If X and X^B are oriented manifolds and AX^B carries the induced orientation, then δ is an isomorphism with $\mathbb{Z}_{(2)}$-coefficients (integers localized at (2)). The orientations yield isomorphisms $H_{n-1}(X^B;\mathbb{Z}) = \mathbb{Z}$, $H^{n-1}(AX^B;\mathbb{Z}_{(2)}) \cong \mathbb{Z}_{(2)}$. The element

$\delta^{-1}D^{-1}i_*(1) \in \mathbb{Z}_{(2)}$ is called the linking number in this case. Reduction mod 2 yields the previously defined linking number.

<u>6.1 Theorem.</u> Let D_{2m} act on a $\mathbb{Z}/2$-homology sphere X of dimension $2n-1$ without fixed points of H. Suppose X^B is a topological manifold. Then X^B has dimension $n-1$ and the linking number of X^B and AX^B is $1 \bmod (2)$.

For smooth actions and m odd this has been shown by MONTGOMERY and YANG [1981]. We see in particular that D_{2m} cannot act freely. We
prove (6.1) by combining ideas from MILNOR [1957], BREDON [1972], and MONTGOMERY - YANG [1981]. See also CAPPELL - SHANESON [1984] for the case $\dim X = 3$.

We use the notation $H = \langle A \rangle$ and $K = \langle B \rangle$ for the subgroup of D_{2m}.

Let M be a K-space and $A : M \to M$ be an arbitrary map. We consider the K-action on $M \times M$ given by $B(x,y) = (y,x)$. The verification of the following lemmas is left to the reader.

<u>6.2 Lemma.</u> The maps

$$f : M \to M \times M, \quad x \mapsto (x,Bx)$$
$$h : M \to M \times M, \quad x \mapsto (Ax,Bx)$$

are K-equivariant. □

<u>6.3 Lemma.</u> Suppose $ABx \neq BAx$ for all $x \in M$. Then f and h have disjoint images. □

<u>6.4 Lemma.</u> Let M be a D_{2m}-space. If $A^2 : M \to M$ has no fixed points, then $ABx \neq BAx$ for all $x \in M$. □

<u>6.5 Lemma.</u> Let M be a D_{2m}-space. The assignments $A(x,y) := (Ax,A^{-1}y)$ and $B(x,y) := (y,x)$ define a D_{2m}-action on $M \times M$. With this action the maps f and h in (6.2) are D_{2m}-equivariant. □

Remark. The action of D_{2m} on $M \times M$ is a special case of the multiplicative induction; see TOM DIECK [1987], I.4, for this construction. This explains (6.2) and (6.5) in a general context.

We now make the following assumptions:
The space M is a $\mathbb{Z}/2$-homology sphere of dimension k. A K-action on M and a $\mathbb{Z}/2$-homology equivalence $A : M \to M$ are given such that $ABx \neq BAx$ for all x. The fixed point set $F = M^K$ is a closed manifold of dimension $l \geq 1$. Then we have:

6.6 Proposition. $k = 2l + 1$.

Proof. Let $D = \operatorname{Im} f$. By (6.2) and (6.3) we have a K-map $h : M \to (M \times M) \setminus D$. The fixed point set of B on $M \times M$ is the diagonal Δ. We thus have an induced map $h : F \to \Delta \setminus (\Delta \cap D)$. We have

6.7 $$F \cap AF = \emptyset,$$
for $y = Ax$ with $x, y \in F$ would imply $ABx = Ax = y = By = BAx$, contradicting our assumption. Consider the projection

6.8 $$p : (M \times M) \setminus D \to M, \quad (x,y) \mapsto x.$$
We need

6.9 Proposition. The map (6.8) is a $\mathbb{Z}/2$-homology equivalence.

Proof. See MILNOR [1957]; BREDON [1972], p.152. □

Using (6.7), we see that we have a commutative diagram (6.10).

6.10 $$\begin{array}{ccc} (M,F) & \xrightarrow{\quad A \quad} & (M, M \setminus F) \\ & {}_{h}\searrow \qquad \nearrow_{p} & \\ & ((M \times M) \setminus D,\ \Delta \setminus \Delta \cap D) & \end{array}$$

The maps in this diagram are $\mathbb{Z}/2$-homology equivalences.

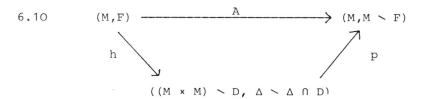

Indeed by (6.9) $p : (M \times M) \setminus D \to M$ is a $\mathbb{Z}/2$-homology equivalence and by inspection $p : \Delta \setminus \Delta \cap D \to M \cap F$ is a homeomorphism. Since $A : M \to M$ is a $\mathbb{Z}/2$-homology equivalence by assumption the same is true for $h : M \to (M \times M) \setminus D$.
By P.A. Smith theory, $h^K : F \to \Delta \setminus \Delta \cap D$ is a $\mathbb{Z}/2$-homolgy equivalence (TOM DIECK [1987], III(4.22)). Thus $A : F \to M \setminus F$ is a $\mathbb{Z}/2$-homology equivalence. Since F is a $\mathbb{Z}/2$-homology sphere (by Smith theory) and a manifold, duality implies that $M \setminus F$ is a $\mathbb{Z}/2$-homology sphere of dimension $k - l - 1$. The existence of the equivalence A shows $l = k - l - 1$. □

6.11 Proposition. Retain the hypotheses of (6.6). Suppose that A is a homeomorphism. Then F and AF are linked in M and the linking number is $1 \bmod (2)$.

Proof. This is a rephrasing of the fact that the inclusion $AF \subset M \setminus F$ induces an isomorphism in $\mathbb{Z}/2$-homology. □

Theorem (6.1) follows from (6.6) and (6.11). Note that the hypotheses of (6.6) and (6.11) are satisfied if D_{2m} acts locally linearly (e.g. smoothly) on a $\mathbb{Z}/2$-homology sphere M such that A^2 has no fixed points.

Remark. Proposition (6.6) could be applied to an action of the infinite dihedral group

$$D_{2\infty} = \langle A, B \mid BAB^{-1} = A^{-1} \rangle \cong \mathbb{Z}/2 * \mathbb{Z}/2.$$

The standard linear representations of D_{2m} are examples for the situation encountered in (6.1); the reader should check this.

We next show how the geometry of representations can be used to obtain arithmetical information.

Let $(d, 2m) = 1$, and $\zeta = \exp(2\pi i/m)$. Let $V(d)$ be the representation of D_{2m} on $\mathbb{R}^2 = \mathbb{C}$ given by

$$A : z \longmapsto \zeta^d z, \quad B : z \longmapsto \bar{z}.$$

The map $f_d : V(1) \longrightarrow V(d)$, $z \longmapsto z^d$ is G-equivariant and induces a G-equivariant map between the unit circles

$$f_d \cdot SV(1) \longrightarrow SV(d).$$

Use the following equivariant triangulation of S^1:
(1) The 0-simplices are the ζ^t, $0 \leq t < 2m$.
(2) The 1-simplices are the arcs in between: $e_0, e_1, \ldots, e_{2m-1}$.

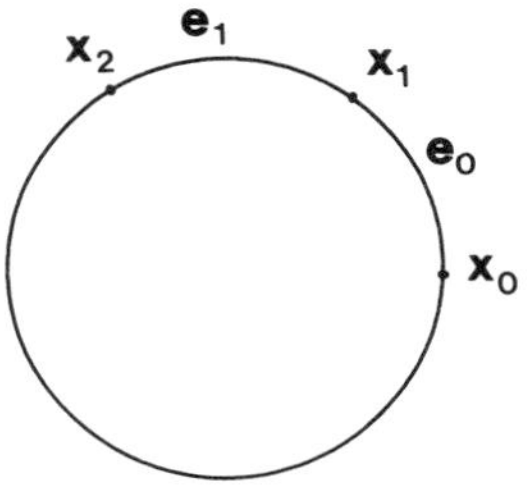

The group D_{2m} acts on the <u>oriented</u> 1-cells of $SV(d)$ as follows:

$$Ae_j = e_{j+2d}, \quad Be_j = -e_{(2m-1)-j}.$$

Let $M(d)$ be the free $\mathbb{Z}$-module with basis $e_0, \ldots, e_{2m-1}$ and this G-action. Then

<u>6.12 Lemma</u>. $M(d)$ is a free $\mathbb{Z}G$-module with basis e_0. □

Of course, $M(d)$ is the module of cellular 1-chains. The map $f_d : SV(1) \longrightarrow SV(d)$ induces a map between these chain groups. It has the following effect on the basis elements:

$$f_d(e_j) = e_{jd} + e_{jd+1} + \ldots + e_{j(d+1)-1}.$$

<u>6.13 Lemma</u>. The cokernel of

$$f_d : M(1) \longrightarrow M(d)$$

is isomorphic to $\mathbb{Z}/d$. The action of $\mathbb{Z}G$ on this cokernel is: $A = \mathrm{id}$, $B = -\mathrm{id}$.

<u>1. Proof</u>. Let $C(f_d) = C_d$ be the mapping cone of the map $f_d : SV(1) \longrightarrow SV(d)$ of degree d. Then

$$\tilde{H}_i(C_d;\mathbb{Z}) = \begin{cases} \mathbb{Z}/d & i = 1 \\ 0 & \text{otherwise.} \end{cases}$$

The action of $\mathbb{Z}G$ on $H_1(C_d)$ is as described. Since f_d is a homeomorphism on the zero-skeleton, we obtain the same homology groups, if we identify the zero-skeleton and the corresponding mapping cone to a point. (By the way: the zero-skeleton is the set of points where G does not act freely.) Note that $H_1(SV(d)/SV(d)^0) \cong M(d)$. The cokernel in question is $H_1(C(f_d)/C(f_d^0)) \cong \mathbb{Z}/d$.

<u>2. Proof</u>. There is, of course, an algebraic proof. One has to show that the determined

$$\begin{vmatrix} \overbrace{1 & 1 & 1 & \dots & 1}^{d} & 0 & \dots & 0 \\ 0 & 1 & 1 & \dots & 1 & 1 & 0 \,.. & 0 \\ \dots\dots & & & & & & & \\ & & & & & & & \end{vmatrix}$$

has absolute value d. It is interesting that the geometry evaluates this determinant without computation. □

Let $\varepsilon : M(d) \longrightarrow \mathbb{Z}/d$ be the augmentation $\varepsilon(\Sigma n_j e_j) = \Sigma n_j \bmod d$.

Then the sequence

$$0 \longrightarrow M(1) \xrightarrow[f_d]{} M(d) \xrightarrow[\varepsilon]{} \mathbb{Z}/d \longrightarrow 0$$

is exact. We thus found a free resolution of the $\mathbb{Z}G$-module $\mathbb{Z}/d_w$ where w refers to the G-action given by $w : G \longrightarrow \mathbb{Z}^*$, $w(A) = 1$, $w(B) = -1$. We rewrite this sequence in terms of standard free modules $\mathbb{Z}G$

$$\begin{array}{ccccc} \mathbb{Z}G & \xrightarrow{\tilde{f}_d} & \mathbb{Z}G & \searrow & \\ \downarrow \cong & & \downarrow \cong & & \mathbb{Z}/d_w \\ M_1 & \xrightarrow[f_d]{} & M_d & \nearrow_{\varepsilon} & \end{array}$$

We have $f_d(e_0) = e_0 + e_1 + \ldots + e_{d-1}$. We thus have to write $e_0 + \ldots + e_{d-1}$ in the form $x(d)e_0$, $x(d) \in \mathbb{Z}G$. The computations simplify if we observe that $z \longmapsto z^d$ generally induces a map $M(l) \longrightarrow M(ld)$. Let $de = 1 \bmod 2m$ and consider

$$M(e) \xrightarrow[f_d]{} M(1) \xrightarrow[\varepsilon]{} \mathbb{Z}/d.$$

We have to write $e_0 + e_1 + \ldots + e_{d-1} = y$ in M_1 as $x(1)e_0$. Let $d = 2l + 1$. Then

$$\begin{aligned} y &= e_0 + e_2 + \ldots + e_{2l} + e_{-1+2} + \ldots + e_{-1+2l} \\ &= e_0 + Ae_0 + \ldots + A^l e_0 - ABe_0 - \ldots - A^l Be_0 \\ &= (1 + A + \ldots + A^l - AB - \ldots - A^l B)e_0 \\ &= x(1)e_0. \end{aligned}$$

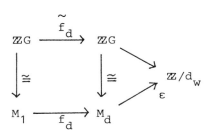

<u>6.14 Proposition</u>. The element $x(1)$ is a unit modulo $\Sigma_w = \Sigma w(g)g$.

<u>Proof</u>. Let $de = 1 + k|G|$. Consider

$$\begin{array}{ccccc} M(1) & \xrightarrow[f_e]{} & M(e) & \xrightarrow[f_d]{} & M(1) \\ & & \underbrace{\qquad\qquad\qquad}_{f_{de}} & & \end{array}$$

The map f_{de} is multiplication with

$$\begin{aligned} e_0 + \ldots + e_{|k|G} &= k(e_0 + \ldots + e_{|G|-1}) + e_0 \\ &= (1 + k\Sigma_w)e_0, \end{aligned}$$

hence $x(1)x(e) = 1 + k\Sigma_w$. □

<u>Remark</u>. Let $\alpha_w : \mathbb{Z}G \longrightarrow \mathbb{Z}, \Sigma n_g g \mapsto \Sigma n_g w(g)$ be the w-augmentation
Then $\alpha_w x(1) = d$.
Using the isomorphism

$$\mathbb{Z}G \longrightarrow \mathbb{Z}G, \quad x = \Sigma n_g g \longmapsto \Sigma w(g) n_g g = \tilde{x}$$

One obtains a resolution of the trivial $\mathbb{Z}G$-module $\mathbb{Z}/d$

$$0 \longrightarrow \mathbb{Z}G \xrightarrow[\tilde{x}(1)]{} \mathbb{Z}G \longrightarrow \mathbb{Z}/d \longrightarrow 0$$

with $\tilde{x}(1) = 1 + A + \ldots A^1 + AB + \ldots + A^1 B$ and $a\tilde{x}(1) = d$.
Using SWAN [1960] one concludes that the modules $\langle d, \Sigma \rangle \subset \mathbb{Z}D_{2m}$ and $\langle d, \Sigma_w \rangle \subset \mathbb{Z}D_{2m}$ are free $\mathbb{Z}D_{2m}$-modules. Here $\langle d, \Sigma \rangle$ is the submodule generated by d and $\Sigma = \Sigma g$.

7. Actions on Brieskorn varieties.

Let $d > 2$ be an odd integer. Let W_d^{2n-1} be the $(2n-1)$-dimensional Brieskorn variety given as the set of common zeros of the equations

$$z_0^d + z_1^2 + \ldots + z_n^2 = 0$$
$$|z_0|^2 + \ldots + |z_n|^2 = 1.$$

This is a smooth submanifold of $\mathbb{C}^{n+1}$. It carries an $O(n)$-action by letting a matrix $A \in O(n)$ act on $(z_1,\ldots,z_n)$ in the standard manner. A homomorphism $\rho : G \longrightarrow O(n)$ makes W_d^{2n-1} into a smooth G-manifold. Regarding $\mathbb{C}^n$ via ρ as a G-representation V we consider W_d^{2n-1} as a G-manifold of $\mathbb{C} \oplus V$ and $S(\mathbb{C} \oplus V)$ and denote it also by

$$W_d(V).$$

Note that the representation V is the complexification of a real representation.
The manifold W_d^{2n-1} has another description as

$$S^{n-1} \times D^n \cup_{\varphi(d)} S^{n-1} \times D^n;$$

the two copies of $S^{n-1} \times D^n$ are identified along their boundary with an $O(n)$-equivariant diffeomorphism

$$\varphi(d) : S^{n-1} \times S^{n-1} \longrightarrow S^{n-1} \times S^{n-1}$$

with mapping degree

$$\begin{pmatrix} 1+d & -d \\ d & 1-d \end{pmatrix} \quad n \text{ even}, \qquad \begin{pmatrix} 0 & 1 \\ 1 & 0 \end{pmatrix} \quad n \text{ odd}.$$

The action of $O(n)$ is the diagonal action. (See BREDON [1972], v. 9.2, p. 275.)
Let $\varphi : S^{n-1} \times S^{n-1} \longrightarrow S^{n-1} \times S^{n-1}$ be any homeomorphism with degree

$$\begin{pmatrix} a & b \\ c & d \end{pmatrix}, \quad b \neq 0.$$

The homology of $M = S^{n-1} \times D^n \cup_{\varphi} S^{n-1} \times D^n$ is computed with the Mayer-Vietoris sequence

$$\longrightarrow H_j(S_1^{n-1} \times S_2^{n-1}) \xrightarrow{\alpha} H_j(S_1^{n-1} \times D_1^n) \oplus H_j(S_2^{n-1} \times D_2^n) \longrightarrow H_j(M) \longrightarrow \;;$$

we have distinguished the two copies of $S^{n-1} \times D^n$ by an index 1 or 2. For $j = n-1$ the map φ is given in terms of the standard basis

$$e_1 = z \times 1,\ e_2 = 1 \times z \in H_{n-1}(S_1^{n-1} \times S_2^{n-1})$$
$$e' = z \times 1 \in H_{n-1}(S_1^{n-1} \times D_1^n),\ e'' = z \times 1 \in H_{n-1}(S_2^{n-1} \times D_2^n)$$

as $\alpha(xe_1 + ye_2) = xe' + (ax + by)e''$ and the matrix

$$\begin{pmatrix} 1 & 0 \\ a & b \end{pmatrix}$$

This yields $H_{n-1}(M) \cong \mathbb{Z}/|b|$ and $H_j(M) = 0$ for $j \neq 0, n-1, 2n-1$.
The cokernel of φ is identified via

$$\varepsilon \cdot \mathbb{Z}e' \oplus \mathbb{Z}e'' \longrightarrow \mathbb{Z}/b, \quad ue' + ve'' \longmapsto v-au.$$

A generator $x \in H_{n-1}(M)$ is represented by e'' hence by the cycle $S_2^{n-1} \times 0$. Since $(a,b) = 1$ the element e' and the cycle

$S_1^{n-1} \times 0$ represents another generator $y = -ax$ of $H_{n-1}(M)$. The manifold M has a linking form

$$\eta : H_{n-1}(M) \times H_{n-1}(M) \longrightarrow \mathbb{Q}/\mathbb{Z}.$$

The value $\eta(-ax,x)$ is given as b^{-1} times the intersection number of $S_1^{n-1} \times 0$ with a bounding chain for $S_2^{n-1} \times 0$. The cycle $t \times S^{n-1}$ is a boundary of $t \times D_1^n$ for $t \in S_1^{n-1}$. This cycle is also given by

$$S^{n-1} \longrightarrow S_2^{n-1} \times D_2^n, \quad s \longmapsto \varphi(0,s)$$

which is $b(S_2^{n-1} \times 0)$. The intersection number of $S_1^{n-1} \times 0$ and $t \times D_1^n$ is 1, since there is a single transverse intersection. Hence

$$\eta(-ax,x) = \frac{1}{b}.$$

In case of the Brieskorn variety we obtain $\eta(-(1+d)x,x) = -\frac{1}{d}$ or, since we may compute modulo d,

$$\eta(x,x) = \frac{1}{d}.$$

Therefore, we have shown

<u>7.1 Proposition</u>. The linking form of W_d^{2n-1} is isomorphic to the standard form

$$\mathbb{Z}/d \times \mathbb{Z}/d \longrightarrow \mathbb{Q}/\mathbb{Z}, \quad (1,1) \longmapsto \frac{1}{d}. \quad \square$$

The action of $O(n)$ on $H_{n-1}(S^{n-1}) = \mathbb{Z}$ is given by the determinant and similarly for the real representation $\rho : G \longrightarrow O(n)$. The determinant $w : G \longrightarrow \mathbb{Z}^*$ gives us a $\mathbb{Z}G$-modul $\mathbb{Z}/d_W \cong H_{n-1}(W)$. Therefore, we obtain

7.2 Proposition. The G-equivariant linking form on $H_{n-1}(W_d(V))$ is isomorphic to

$$\mathbb{Z}/d_W \times \mathbb{Z}/d_W \longrightarrow \mathbb{Q}G/\mathbb{Z}G, \qquad (1,1) \longmapsto \frac{1}{d} \Sigma_W$$

with $\Sigma_W = \sum_{g \in G} w(g)g$. □

Our next result states that representing cycles for $H_{n-1}(W_d^{2n-1})$ may be chosen disjoint to Brieskorn subvarieties. The diffeomorphism

$$\varphi(d) : S^{n-1} \times S^{n-1} \longrightarrow S^{n-1} \times S^{n-1}$$

preserves the standard spheres $S^{k-1} \subset S^{n-1}$, $(x_1,\ldots,x_k) \longmapsto (x_1,\ldots,x_k,0,\ldots,0)$ and yields

$$\varphi(d) : S^{k-1} \times S^{k-1} \longrightarrow S^{k-1} \times S^{k-1}$$

and an inclusion

$$W_d^{2k-1} \subset W_d^{2n-1}.$$

7.3 Proposition. A generator of $H_{n-1}(W_d^{2n-1})$ can be represented by a spherical cycle which is disjoint to W_d^{2k-1}.

Proof. The cycle $S_2^{n-1} \times 0$ in W_d^{2n-1} is also represented by $S_2^{n-1} \times t$, $t \in D_2^n$ for all t. If $t \in D_2^n \setminus D_2^k$, then the cycle is disjoint to W_d^{2k-1}. □

We actually need a slight refinement of Proposition (7.3) in order to apply it to group actions and the varieties $W_d(V)$. The singular set of the action is the union of the proper fixed point sets

$$\bigcup_{G \supset H \neq 1} W_d(V)^H = \cup\, W_d(V^H).$$

Let U denote $\mathbb{R}^n$ with the G-action given by the real representation $\rho : G \longrightarrow O(n)$. Then $W_d(V^H)$, as a submanifold of $W_d(V)$, can be identified with

$$S(U^H) \times D(U^H) \cup_{\varphi(d)} S(U^H) \times D(U^H).$$

Therefore, if we choose the t in the proof of Proposition 3 away from the singular set $\bigcup_{H\neq 1} D(U^H)$ in $D(U)$ we obtain

7.4 Proposition. A generator of $H_{n-1}(W_d(V))$ can be represented by a spherical cycle which is disjoint to the singular set. □

We want to turn the G-manifolds $W_d(V)$ into spheres by applying equivariant framed surgery. Note that the definition of $W_d(V)$ as a submanifold of $\mathbb{C} \oplus V$, as the pre-image of the regular value $(0,1)$ of the G-invariant function

$$\mathbb{C} \oplus V \longrightarrow \mathbb{C} \oplus \mathbb{R}, \; (z_0,\ldots,z_n) \longmapsto (z_0^d+\ldots+z_n^2, \; \Sigma|z_i|^2),$$

induces a canonical equivariant framing (= tangential structure)

$$TW_d(V) \oplus \mathbb{C} \oplus \mathbb{R} \longrightarrow \mathbb{C} \oplus V.$$

Since $W_d(V)$ is highly connected and $H_{n-1}(W_d(V)) \cong \mathbb{Z}/d_W$ we have to perform surgery on linking forms. We need the following slight extension of Theorem 5.6 in WALL [1966] which we prove in section 9.

7.5 Theorem. Let W^{2n-1} be a highly connected smooth framed G-manifold. Suppose $H_{n-1}(W)$ is a torsion subgroup. Suppose the elements in $H_{n-1}(W)$ can be represented by spherical cycles which are disjoint to the singular set. Suppose the equivariant linking form on $H_{n-1}(W)$ has a free resolution in the sense of WALL [1966]. Then we can perform equivariant framed surgery on W^{2n-1} leaving the singular set fixed and turning W^{2n-1} into a sphere. □

In the next section we describe a free resolution of the linking form of Proposition (7.2), provided $v \in (\mathbb{Z}G/\Sigma_W)^*$ is a unit such that $\alpha(v)^2 = \pm d \mod 8|G|$, where $\alpha(\Sigma n_g g) = \Sigma n_g w(g)$ is the w-augmentation.

I list a few cases to which the considerations above can be applied. Let $D_{2m} = \langle D, S \mid D^m = 1 = S^2, SDS^{-1} \rangle$ be the dihedral group of order $2m$. Then $D_{2m} \subset O(2)$ is the standard representation U. Let U^n be the direct sum of n copies of U and $V = V^n$ its complexification. The fixed point set V^S has complex dimension n. If $n \geq 3$ is odd, then $W_d(V^S)$ is homeomorphic to a sphere (BRIESKORN [1966]). Also it is known by (6.14) that each element in $\mathbb{Z}/2m^*$ appears as $\alpha(v)$ of a unit $\mathbb{Z}D_{2m}/\Sigma_w^*$. Therefore, Theorem (7.5) yields in this case

<u>7.6 Theorem</u>. There exists a smooth D_{2m}-action on a sphere S^{8k+3} (with some differentiable structure) such that the fixed point sets of the involutions of D_{2m} (which are spheres of dimension $4k+1$) have linking number d, provided $\pm d$ is a square mod $8m$ (and prime to m).

<u>Proof</u>. One applies Theorem (7.5) to $W_d(V^n)$ for $n = 2k+1$, $k \geq 1$, to turn this manifold into a sphere without changing the fixed point sets of involutions. That the fixed points set have linking number d is shown in TOM DIECK [1986]. □

Other interesting examples occur for the group $\mathbb{Z}/2 \times \mathbb{Z}/2 = H \times K$. Here we take the representation $V = V_1 \oplus V_2$, where V_1 has kernel K and V_2 has kernel H. If the dimensions of V_1 and V_2 are odd, then $W_d(V)^K = W_d(V_1)$ and $W_d(V)^H = W_d(V_2)$ are spheres and $W_d(V)$ can be turned into a sphere provided $d \equiv \pm 1 \mod 8$. Thus we have

<u>7.7 Theorem</u>. There exist smooth actions of $\mathbb{Z}/2 \times \mathbb{Z}/2 = H \times K$ on $S^{4(k+h)+1} = \Sigma$ (with some differentiable structure) such that $\Sigma^H \cong S^{2h+1}$, $\Sigma^K \cong S^{2k+1}$ and such that Σ^H and Σ^K have linking number d in Σ, provided $d \equiv \pm 1 \mod 8$. □

Remark. Note that the constructions above yield fixed point sets S^1 and S^{2k+1}, $k \geq 2$, linking in S^{2k+3}. This is interesting because one has a codimension 2 situation. So it is interesting to know the types of knots that can occur as such linking fixed point situation.

The Brieskorn varieties are relevant for the problem of geometric multiples of representations. We are going to explain this problem.

A more invariant description of the Brieskorn varieties can be given as follows. Let W be an n-dimensional real vector space with inner product $\langle -,- \rangle$. On $W \oplus_{\mathbb{R}} \mathbb{C} = U$ we have a linear form

$$b(w_1 \otimes z_1, w_2 \otimes z_2) = \langle w_1, w_2 \rangle z_1, z_2$$

and an Hermitian form

$$\langle w_1 \otimes z_1, w_2 \otimes z_2 \rangle = z_1 \langle w_1, w_2 \rangle \bar{z}_2.$$

We define

$$W_d(U) = \{ (z,u) \in \mathbb{C} \oplus U \mid z^d + b(u,u) = 0, \ |z|^2 + \langle u,u \rangle = 1 \}.$$

If W carries an orthogonal action of G, then we obtain induced actions on U and $W_d(U)$. From the definition is now obvious that

$$W_d(W)^H = W_d(W^H).$$

We have an equivariant map

7.8 $\qquad \varphi : W_d(U) \longrightarrow S(U), \quad (z,u) \longmapsto u/|u|.$

It is easy to see

7.9 Lemma. φ has degree d. □

We set

$$V_d^t(U) = \{(z,u) \mid z^d + b(u,u) = t\}.$$
$$W_d^t(U) = V_d^t(U) \cap \{(z,u) \mid |z|^2 + \langle u,u\rangle = t\}.$$

<u>7.10 Lemma</u>. For all sufficiently small t the G-manifold $W_d^t(U)$ is G-diffeomorphic to $W_d(U)$.

<u>Proof</u>. See HIRZEBRUCH - MAYER [1968], p.103.

For $t > 0$ the manifold $V_d^t(U)$ has no singularities and $W_d^t(U)$ is the boundary of the G-manifold

$$C_d^t(U) = V_d^t(U) \cap \{(z,u) \mid |z|^2 + \langle u,u\rangle \leq 1\}.$$

Let $t < 1$. The d points $P_\omega = (\omega,0)$ with $\omega^d = 1$ are contained in the interior of $C_d^t(U)$ and they are contained in the fixed point set of the G-action.

<u>7.11 Lemma</u>. The tangential representations of G at P_ω are isomorphic to U.

<u>Proof</u>. The interior of $C_d^t(U)$ carries a complex structure by its very definition. The group G acts by complex automorphisms. Therefore, the tangential representations are complex representations.

Fix ω such that $\omega^d = t$. Let $U = \mathbb{C}^n$ with coordinates $(z_1,\ldots,z_n)$. In a connected neighbourhood $U_0 \subset \{(z_1,\ldots,z_n) \mid |z_1^2 +\ldots+ z_n^2| < 1\}$ of $0 \in U_0$ there exists a holomorphic function $\alpha : U_0 \longrightarrow \mathbb{C}$ with $\alpha(0) = \omega$ and $\alpha(z_1,\ldots,z_n)^d = t - (z_1^2 +\ldots+ z_n^2)$. The inequality $|\alpha(z_1,\ldots,z_n)|^2 + |z_1|^2 +\ldots+ |z_n|^2 < 1$ is satisfied for $z = 0$ and hence in a sufficiently small U_0. We obtain a map

$$A : U_0 \longrightarrow C_d^t, \quad u = (z_1,\ldots,z_n) \longmapsto (\alpha(u),u),$$

which is G-equivariant. It is a local coordinate system about

$(\omega,0,\ldots,0)$ since the projection with $C_d^t \to U, (z,u) \mapsto u$ is the identity. □

If we cut out small G-invariant disks about the fixed points in C_d^t we obtain

<u>7.12 Corollary</u>. The manifolds C_d^t yields a G-bordism between $W_d^t(U) \cong W_d(U)$ and $dS(U)$, the disjoint union of d copies of $S(U)$.

The general problem of geometric d-folds of representations U is the question:
When is $dS(U)$ G-bordant to a representation form? We would like thebordism to introduce no new isotropy groups.
Moreover, since $dS(U)$ has a natural mapping to $S(U)$ of degree d on all non-empty fixed point sets, we would like to extend this map over the bordism. It turns out, that the bordism (7.12) is actually a bordism to the map (7.8). Theorem (7.6) can be read as a solution of the problem of d-folds (for certain d) in case of the dihedral groups.

8. Resolution of linking forms.

The section contains the algebra needed for (7.6). We use the following notation.

G a finite group

$w : G \longrightarrow \{\pm 1\} = \mathbb{Z}^*$ a homomorphism

$\mathbb{Z}G$ group ring with involution $x = \Sigma n_g g \mapsto x^* = \Sigma n_g g^{-1}$

$\Sigma_w = \Sigma w(g)g$; then $\Sigma_w^* = \Sigma_w$.

$v \in \mathbb{Z}G$ with image $v \in (\mathbb{Z}G/\Sigma_w)^*$ a unit

$\alpha = \alpha_w : \mathbb{Z}G \longrightarrow \mathbb{Z}$, $\Sigma n_g g \longmapsto \Sigma n_g w(g)$ the w-augmentation.

$\mathbb{Z}_w$ is $\mathbb{Z}$ with G-action given by w; then $\alpha_w : \mathbb{Z}G \longrightarrow \mathbb{Z}_w$ is $\mathbb{Z}G$-linear.

$0 < d \in \mathbb{Z}$, $(d,|G|) = 1$.

The reader is asked to verify

8.1 Lemma. The diagram

$$\begin{array}{ccc} \mathbb{Z}G & \xrightarrow{\alpha_w} & \mathbb{Z} \\ \downarrow & & \downarrow \\ \mathbb{Z}G/\Sigma_w & \xrightarrow{\alpha_w} & \mathbb{Z}/|G| \end{array}$$

is a pullback of rings. □

Let us assume $\alpha_w(v)^2 = \pm d \bmod |G|$ and write $\alpha_w(v)^2 - kl|G| = \pm d$, with $k,l \in \mathbb{Z}$, $(k,d) = 1$. Consider the (2,2)-matrix over $\mathbb{Z}G$

$$C = \begin{pmatrix} k & v \\ v^* & l\Sigma_w \end{pmatrix}.$$

It satisfies ${}^tC^* = C$, hence is hermitian. The matrix is even, i.e. of the form $C = B + {}^tB^*$ if and only if k and l are even.

Consider the $\mathbb{Z}G$-linear map

$$\eta : \mathbb{Z}G^2 \longrightarrow \mathbb{Z}/d_w, \quad (a,b) \longmapsto \alpha(a)\alpha(v) - \alpha(b)k \bmod d.$$

8.2 Proposition. The sequence

$$0 \longrightarrow \mathbb{Z}G^2 \xrightarrow[C]{} \mathbb{Z}G^2 \xrightarrow[\eta]{} \mathbb{Z}/d_w \longrightarrow 0$$

is exact.

Proof. From $(k,d) = 1$ we see immediately that η is surjective. An element (a,b) in the image of C has the form

8.3 $$\begin{aligned} kx + vy &= a \\ v^*x + l\Sigma_w y &= b \end{aligned} \qquad x,y \in \mathbb{Z}G.$$

If we apply η we obtain

$$\begin{aligned} &(k\alpha(x) + \alpha(v)\alpha(y))\alpha(v) - k(\alpha(v)\alpha(x) + l|G|\alpha(y)) \\ &= (\alpha(v)^2 - kl|G|)\alpha(y) = \pm d\alpha(y) \equiv 0 \bmod d. \end{aligned}$$

Now suppose that $\eta(a,b) = 0$. We show that (8.3) has a unique solution (x,y). We use Lemma (8.1) and show that there exist unique solutions over $\mathbb{Z}G/\Sigma_w$ and $\mathbb{Z}$ which fit together over $\mathbb{Z}/|G|$.

Solutions over $\mathbb{Z}$. We apply α to (8.3) and solve for $\alpha(x)$ and $\alpha(y)$. We obtain:

8.4 $$\alpha(y) = \pm d^{-1}(\alpha(a)\alpha(v) - \alpha(b)k)$$

which is an integer because $\eta(a,b) = 0$;

8.5 $$\alpha(x) = \pm d^{-1}(\alpha(b)\alpha(v) - \alpha(a)l|G|).$$

We have to show that $\alpha(b)\alpha(v) - \alpha(a)l|G| \equiv 0 \mod d$. Since $(k,d) = 1$ we can multiply by k and obtain

$$\begin{aligned} & k\alpha(b)\alpha(v) - \alpha(a)kl|G| \\ \equiv\ & k\alpha(b)\alpha(v) - \alpha(a)\alpha(v)^2 \\ \equiv\ & (k\alpha(b) - \alpha(a)\alpha(b))\alpha(v) \equiv 0. \end{aligned}$$

<u>Solutions over</u> $\mathbb{Z}G/\Sigma_w$. We have the system

$$\begin{aligned} kx + vy &= a \\ v^*x \quad &= b \end{aligned}$$

with units v, v^*. The solution necessarily has the form

$$x = (v^*)^{-1}b, \; y = v^{-1}(a-k(v^*)^{-1}b).$$

It is easy to verify that the solutions fit together over $\mathbb{Z}/G$. □

We now determine the linking form over $\mathbb{Z}/d_w$ which is induced by C. For the following computations note that

8.6 $$\begin{aligned} x\Sigma_w &= \alpha(x)\Sigma_w \quad \text{for } x \in \mathbb{Z}G \\ \Sigma_w^2 &= |G|\Sigma_w. \end{aligned}$$

The matrix C maps $(v\Sigma_w, -k\Sigma_w)$ to $(0, \pm d\Sigma_w)$. Since $(k,d) = 1 = (d,|G|)$ and $\eta(0, \pm \Sigma_w) = \mp k|G|$ we see that $\eta(0, \pm \Sigma_w)$ is a generator x of $\mathbb{Z}_w/d$.
Using this generator we obtain for the induced linking form $\langle -,- \rangle$ on $\mathbb{Z}/d_w$ the value

8.7 $$\langle x,x \rangle = \frac{1}{d}(0, \pm \Sigma_w) \begin{pmatrix} v\Sigma_w \\ -k\Sigma_w \end{pmatrix} = \frac{\mp k|G|}{d} \Sigma_w.$$

We also note that $\langle x,x \rangle = \frac{a}{d}\Sigma_w$ and $\langle x,x \rangle = \frac{at^2}{d}\Sigma_w$ are isomorphic forms; also, we can change a in its class mod d. Using this and (8.7) we obtain

<u>8.8 Proposition</u>. Suppose $\alpha(v)^2 \equiv \pm d \bmod 8|G|$, say $\alpha(v)^2 - 8m|G| = \pm d$. Then the even matrix

$$C = \begin{pmatrix} \mp 2m & v \\ v^* & 4\Sigma_w \end{pmatrix}$$

yields a resolution of the linking form
$q : \mathbb{Z}/d \longrightarrow \mathbb{Q}G/\mathbb{Z}G$, $1 \longmapsto \frac{1}{d}\,\Sigma_w$.

<u>Proof</u>. By the remarks above the following elements yield isomorphic forms

$$\frac{2m|G|}{d}, \quad \frac{2m|G|\cdot 2^2}{d}, \quad \frac{\alpha(v)^2}{d}, \quad \frac{1}{d}. \quad \square$$

<u>Remark</u>. If $|G|$ is even, then $\pm d$ is a square mod $8|G|$ if and only if it is a square mod $4|G|$. Since we can replace $\alpha(v)$ with $\alpha(v) + s\Sigma w$ we can arrive at an equation $\alpha(v)^2 - 8m|G| = \pm d$ with $(2m,d) = 1$. If one does not look for an even matrix, then the condition $\alpha(v)^2 \equiv \pm d \bmod |G|$ suffices in order to find a resolution.

9. Surgery and linking forms

In this section we prove Theorem (7.5). The proof is based on WALL [1966], V. It demonstrates in a simple and explicit manner the process of surgery.

Let $M = M^{2k+1}$ be a closed $(2k+1)$-dimensional oriented G-manifold. Let

9.1 $$\varphi_1, \dots \varphi_r : G \times S^k \times D^{k+1} \longrightarrow M$$

be disjoint G-embeddings. We use them to perform equivariant surgery. Let M' be the result. The passage from M to M' can change homology only in dimensions k and $k+1$. In order to analyse the effect on homology we use the following diagram of KERVAIRE and MILNOR [1963]. Let $U = \bigcup_{i=1}^{r} \varphi_i(G \times S^k \times \mathring{D}^{k+1})$. Then we have the diagram

9.2
$$\begin{array}{ccccccc}
 & & H_{k+1}(M', M' \setminus U') & & & & \\
 & & \downarrow{\scriptstyle d'} & & & & \\
H_{k+1}(M, M \setminus U) & \xrightarrow{d} & H_k(M-U) & \xrightarrow{i} & H_k(M) & \longrightarrow & 0 \\
 & & \downarrow{\scriptstyle i'} & & & & \\
 & & H_k(M') & & & & \\
 & & \downarrow & & & & \\
 & & 0 & & & &
\end{array}$$

The maps d, i and d', i' belong to the exact homology sequences of $(M, M \setminus U)$ and $(M', M' \setminus U')$. Note that $M \setminus U = M' \setminus U'$.

9.3 Assumption. $H_k(M)$ and $H_{k-1}(M)$ are torsion groups. Then duality and universal coefficient formula imply $H_{k+1}(M) = 0$.

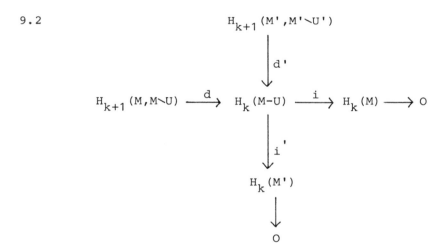

The group

$$H_{k+1}(M, M \smallsetminus U) \cong H_{k+1}(\coprod G \times S^r \times (D^{r+1}, S^r))$$

is a free $\Lambda = \mathbb{Z}G$ module with basis $u_1, \dots, u_r$ represented by the cycles

$$(e \times 1 \times D^{k+1}, \; e \times 1 \times S^k),$$

$1 \in S^k$ a base point. The element $d(u_i) = x_i$ is represented by $\varphi_i(e \times 1 \times S^k)$. Similarly $H_{k+1}(M', M' \smallsetminus U')$ is a free Λ-module with basis $u_1', \dots, u_r'$ and $d'(u_i') = x_i'$ is represented by $\varphi_i(e \times S^k \times 1)$.

The aim is to arrange the surgery in such a way that $H_k(M')=0$. The exactness properties of (9.2) yield:

$$\begin{aligned} H_k(M)/\mathrm{im}(id') &\cong H_k(M \smallsetminus U)/(\mathrm{im}(d) + \mathrm{im}(d')) \\ &\cong H_k(M')/\mathrm{im}(i'd). \end{aligned}$$

If $H_k(M') = 0$, then id' is surjective. Therefore, we make the further

9.4 Assumption. id' is surjective.
This assumption concerns the homological properties of the embeddings φ_i: the elements x_i' have to generate $H_k(M)$.
Under these assumptions we have

9.5 $H_k(M') = 0 \iff i'd = 0 \iff \mathrm{im}(d) \subset \mathrm{im}(d')$. □

9.6 Lemma. $H_k(M \smallsetminus U)$ is torsion free.
A proof of (9.6) is based on duality, universal coefficient formula and the assumptions and will be left to the reader.

As a consequence we see that d is a rational isomorphism. We can use $x_1, \dots, x_r$ as $\mathbb{Q}G$-basis of $H_k(M \smallsetminus U) \otimes \mathbb{Q}$. We obtain relations

9.7 $x'_i = \sum_j c_{ij} x_j \quad , \quad c_{ij} \in \mathbb{Q}G.$

9.8 Lemma. $H_k(M') \otimes \mathbb{Q} = 0$ if and only if the matrix (c_{ij}) is invertible over $\mathbb{Q}G$. If this is the case then $H_{k+1}(M') = 0$ and d' is injective. □

Starting with arbitrary embeddings φ_i satisfying the assumptions above we will, in general, not achieve $H_k(M') = 0$. We therefore look for new embeddings

$$\tilde{\varphi}_1, \ldots, \tilde{\varphi}_r : G \times S^n \times D^{n+1} \longrightarrow M$$

with the following properties.

9.9 There exists an open G-subset $W \subset M$, such that $U \subset W \supset \tilde{U}$ and the inclusions induce isomorphisms

$$H_k(M \setminus U) \xleftarrow{\cong} H_k(M \setminus W) \xrightarrow{\cong} H_k(M \setminus \tilde{U})$$

which we regard as identifications.

9.10 We have

$$\tilde{x}'_i = x'_i + \sum_j \varsigma_{ij} x_j$$

with suitable $\varsigma_{ij} \in \Lambda$. Moreover $\tilde{x}_i = x_i$.

Let M'' be the result of doing surgery with the $\tilde{\varphi}_i$. We want to find conditions on the ς_{ij} which ensure $H_k(M'') = 0$. We must look for a relation of the form

9.11 $x_k = \sum_l a_{kl} \tilde{x}'_l \quad , \quad a_{kl} \in \Lambda.$

By (9.7) and (9.10) we have

$$\tilde{x}'_i = \sum_j (c_{ij} + \varsigma_{ij}) x_j .$$

Therefore

9.12 $(a_{ij})^{-1} = (c_{ij} + \underset{\sim}{c}_{ij})$.

In order to see whether we can satisfy (9.12) we need the geometric significance of the coefficients c_{ij}.

9.13 Lemma. Let $c_{ij} = \sum_{g \in G} c_{ij}(g)g$. Then $c_{ij}(g)$ is the linking number

$$w(g)v(\varphi_i(e \times S^k \times 1), \varphi_j(g \times S^k \times 0))$$

where v denotes linking number and $w(g) \in \{+1,-1\}$ is the orientation character of the g-action on M.

Proof. The $\mathbb{Q}$-module $H_k(M \smallsetminus U;\mathbb{Q})$ has the basis $[\varphi_j(g \times 1 \times S^k)]$. Given a manifold L embedded in $M \smallsetminus U$, then by definition the linking number of L with $[\varphi_j(g \times 1 \times S^k)]$ is the coefficient of L of this basis element. This requires the embedding $\varphi_j : g \times S^k \times D^{k+1} \longrightarrow M$ to be orientation preserving. We assume this to be the case for $g = e$. □

We recall the definition of the equivariant linking form

$$\lambda : H_k(M) \times H_k(M) \longrightarrow \mathbb{Q}G/\mathbb{Z}G$$
$$\lambda(x,y) = \sum_{g \in G} v(x,g^{-1}y)g.$$

It has the following properties

$$\lambda(x,hy) = \lambda(x,y)(w(h)h^{-1})$$
$$\lambda(hx,y) = h\lambda(x,y)$$
$$\lambda(x,y) = (-1)^{k+1}\,\overline{\lambda(y,x)}.$$

We use the involution $x = \Sigma a_g g \mapsto \bar{x} = \Sigma w(g)a_g g^{-1}$ on the group ring and the commutation rule $v(x,y) = (-1)^{|x|\cdot|y|+1}\, v(y,x)$.

A free resolution of this form consists of a surjective homomorphism

$$\pi : \Lambda^r \longrightarrow H_k(M)$$

of $\mathbb{Z}G$-modules and an (r,r)-matrix (a_{ij}) with intries in $\mathbb{Z}G$ which is invertible over $\mathbb{Q}G$ and satisfies:

$$a_{ij} = (-1)^{k+1}\, \overline{a_{ji}}$$

$$\lambda(\pi(x_i),\ \pi(y_i)) \equiv (y_i)^t (\bar{a}_{ij})^{-1} (\bar{x}_j)^t$$

modulo $\mathbb{Z}G$.

We can now state the main result.

9.14 Theorem. Let $k \geq 1$ and $H_k(M;\mathbb{Q}) = 0 = \tilde{H}_{k-1}(M;\mathbb{Q})$. Assume $M \setminus M_s$, M_s union of proper fixed point sets, is connected. The linking form on $H_k(M)$ has a resolution $(\pi, (a_{ij}))$. There exist embeddings

$$\varphi_1, \ldots, \varphi_r : G \times S^k \times D^{k+1} \longrightarrow M$$

such that

$$\Lambda^r \ni (y_1, \ldots, y_r) \longmapsto i\left(\sum_{i=1}^{r} y_i x_i'\right) \in H_k(M)$$

is the map π. Then there exist embeddings $\tilde{\varphi}_1, \ldots, \tilde{\varphi}_r$ such that surgery with these embeddings leads to M'' with $H_k(M'') = 0$.

We should point out that (9.14) deals with the simplest situation. We do not consider framings or tangential structures.

Proof. Because of (9.13) we have

$$c_{ij} \equiv \lambda(x_i', x_j') \bmod \mathbb{Z}G.$$

Set $(a_{ij})^{-1} = (b_{ij})$ and $c_{ij} + \varsigma_{ij} = b_{ij}$.

If we can find embeddings $\tilde{\varphi}_j$ such that (9.10) is satisfied then also (9.11) and (9.12) and therefore $H_k(M'') = 0$. Hence it remains to prove the following result. □

9.15 Theorem. Given any matrix (ς_{ij}) we can find embeddings $\tilde{\varphi}_1,\ldots,\tilde{\varphi}_r$ such that (9.9) and (9.10) hold.

Proof. In order to find $\tilde{\varphi}_1 : G \times S^k \times D^{k+1} \longrightarrow M$ with suitable properties we first choose the embedding of $e \times S^k \times 0$, then show that it extends to an embedding of $e \times S^k \times D^{k+1}$ and finally by equivariance to an embedding of $G \times S^k \times D^{k+1}$. Let $\tilde{x}_1' = x_1' + \sum\limits_j \varsigma_j\, x_j = x_1' + \sum\limits_{j,g} \varsigma_j(g) g\, x_j$. The homology classes x_1' and $g\, x_j$ are represented by spheres which are pairwise disjoint, namely: x_1' by $\varphi_1(e \times S^k \times 0)$ and $g\, x_j$ by a small normal sphere to $\varphi_j(g \times S^k \times 0)$, e.g. by $\varphi_j(g \times t \times S^k)$, $t \in S^k$. All these spheres have trivial normal bundle. We obtain a submanifold which represents $\tilde{x}_1'$ by taking $\varphi_1(e \times S^k \times 0)$ and $\varsigma_j(g)$ disjoint copies $\varphi_j(g \times t_\nu \times S^k)$. In case $\varsigma_j(g) < 0$ one has to change the orientation. If all these spheres are contained in an open connected G-subset $W \subset M \setminus M_s$, we can perform connected sum along paths (piping) in order to obtain an embedded sphere S^k with trivial normal bundle representing $\tilde{x}_1'$. In order to achieve that $G \times S^k$ is still embedded one uses small deformations (transversality theorem). This process is now applied to each $\tilde{x}'_j$. The set W is obtained by enlarging U slightly and connecting the components again by piping. □

10. Stably linear homotopy representations.

A homotopy representation X is called stably linear if there exist representations V and W and a G-homotopy equivalence

10.1 $$h : SW \longrightarrow X * SV.$$

We have seen in section 5 that a homotopy representation of a cyclic group is always stably linear. We want to use (10.1) as the starting point for the construction of tangential structures on X. We compose h with the projection

10.2 $$p : X * SV \longrightarrow (X * SV)/SV \cong (X \times V)^+$$

where $(X \times V)^+ = (X \times V) \cup \{\infty\}$ with a topology making it homeomorphic to $(X \times DV)/(X \times SV)$. (This is the Thom space of the trivial bundle $X \times V \longrightarrow X$.)

10.3 Problem. Under which conditions is

$$F = ph : SW \longrightarrow (X \times V)^+$$

G-homotopic to a map which is transverse to $X \times 0$?

Suppose F is transverse. Let $M = F^{-1}(X \times 0)$ and let $f : M \longrightarrow X$ be the restriction of F. Thus we have a commutative diagram

10.4 $$\begin{array}{ccc} SW & \xrightarrow{F} & (X \times V)^+ \\ \uparrow & & \uparrow \\ M & \xrightarrow[f]{} & X \end{array}$$

We assume that X, V and W are oriented. Then $X * SV$ carries an induced orientation. Also, M is orientable, and with correct choice of orientation we have

10.5 Lemma. degree f = degree h.

Proof. Let U be a suitable tabular neighbourhood of $M \subset SW$.

Let $q : SW \longrightarrow SW/SW \setminus U$ be the collaps map. By transversality, the normal bundle of M in SW is induced from the normal bundle of X in $X \times V$. We can assume that F has up to G-homotopy the form

$$SW \xrightarrow{q} SW/SW \setminus U \xrightarrow{\varphi} (X \times V)^+$$

where $\varphi : U \longrightarrow X \times V$ is a bundle map over f. Let $m = \dim M$, $m + k = \dim SW$ and consider the following commutative diagram.

$$\begin{array}{ccc}
H^{m+k}(SW) & \xleftarrow{h^*} & H^{m+k}(X * SV) \\
\cong \uparrow q^* & & \cong \uparrow p^* \\
H^{m+k}(SW/SW \setminus U) & \xleftarrow{\varphi^*} & H^{m+k}((X \times V)^+) \\
\uparrow (1) & & \uparrow (2) \\
H^m(M) & \xleftarrow{f^*} & H^m(X)
\end{array}$$

The maps (1) and (2) are Thom isomorphisms. The lemma follows by inspection of the diagram. □

We can take H-fixed points in (10.4) and by the arguments above we obtain degree f^H = degree h^H, since transversality still holds.

In particular, if h is a map with degree function of constant value one (hence a G-homotopy equivalence), then $f : M \longrightarrow X$ has constant degree one. Having found a suitable map f we ask:

<u>10.6 Problem</u>. Can f be covered by a tangential map

$$\begin{array}{ccc}
TM \oplus k\varepsilon & \longrightarrow & \eta \\
\downarrow & & \downarrow \\
M & \xrightarrow{f} & X
\end{array}$$

for some G-vector bundle η over X ?

By transversality, we have the relations

$$10.7 \quad (TM \oplus \varepsilon) \oplus V \cong (TM \oplus \varepsilon) \oplus \nu(M,SW) \cong (TSW \oplus \varepsilon)|M \cong W$$

(ν normal bundle, V trivial bundle with fibre V).
Therefore, it is reasonable to look for a relation

$$10.8 \qquad \eta \oplus V \cong W$$

for a suitable bundle η over X. This would imply

$$10.9 \qquad f^*\eta \oplus V \cong W.$$

Suppose (10.9) determines the bundle $f^*\eta$ uniquely. Then (10.7) and (10.9) would provide us with a bundle map $TM \oplus \varepsilon \longrightarrow \eta$ over f.

Remark. We point out that (10.1) does not determine the representations V,W uniquely. Only the G-homotopy type of SV and SW matters. The existence of a relation (10.9) can depend on making suitable choices of V and W.

We now give conditions under which (10.3) and (10.6) can be solved.

Let Z be a G-complex. The existence of a relation $\eta \oplus V \cong W$ between bundles over Z is equivalent to the existence of a bundle epimorphism $Z \times W \longrightarrow Z \times V$. Let $\mathrm{Epi}(W,V)$ be the space of linear epimorphisms. This space carries a G-action by conjugation

$$(g\alpha)(r) = g\alpha(g^{-1}v).$$

By adjunction, bundle epimorphisms $Z \times W \longrightarrow Z \times V$ corresponds to G-maps

$$Z \longrightarrow \mathrm{Epi}(W,V).$$

The existence and homotopy classification of such G-maps can be attacked by obstruction theory. One uses induction over orbit bundles in the frame-work of TOM DIECK [1987], I.7.

Suppose there is a given G-map

$$GZ^{>H} \longrightarrow Epi(W,V).$$

Then the obstructions to extending it over GZ^H lie in groups

$$H^{r+1}(Z^H/NH,\ Z^{>H}/NH;\ \pi_r Epi(W,V)^H).$$

These obstruction groups vanish, if

10.10 $\quad \pi_j Epi(W,V)^H = 0 \quad$ for $\quad j < \dim Z^H$.

Thus we have:

<u>10.11 Proposition</u>. There exists a G-map $Z \longrightarrow Epi(W,V)$ provided (10.10) holds for each isotropy group H of Z. The G-homotopy class of this map is uniquely determined provided (10.10) holds for $j \leq \dim Z^H$. □

We need to know the connectivity of the spaces $Epi(W,V)^H$. This is the subspace of the H-linear maps $Hom_H(W,V)$ consisting of epimorphisms.

Let $Irr(H,\mathbb{R})$ be the set of irreducible $\mathbb{R}H$-modules. Write

$$res_H W = \oplus\ w(A)A, \quad res_H V = \oplus\ v(A)A$$

with A running through $Irr(H,\mathbb{R})$ (see BRÖCKER - TOM DIECK [1985], II.6). Then $Hom_H(W,V)$ is non-empty if and only if

10.12 $\quad w(A) \geq v(A) \quad$ for all $\quad A \in Irr(H,\mathbb{R})$.

By the Schur-Lemma we have a canonical splitting

$$Epi_H(W,V) \cong \oplus\ Epi_H(w(A)A,\ v(A)A)$$

and moreover $Epi_H(w(A)A,\ v(A)A)$ is homeomorphic to the Stiefel manifold

10.13 $V_{v(A)}(D(A)^{w(A)})$

of $v(A)$-frames in $D(A)^{w(A)}$. Here $D(A)$ is the endomorphism space of A and is $\mathbb{R}, \mathbb{C}$, or $\mathbb{H}$. The connectivity of the space (10.13) is given by

10.14 $d(A)(w(A) - v(A))$, $d(A) = \dim_{\mathbb{R}} D(A)$, for $v(A) > 0$.

Thus we have

<u>10.15 Proposition</u>. $\mathrm{Epi}(W,V)^H \neq \emptyset$ if and only if $w(A)-v(A) \geq 0$ for all $A \in \mathrm{Irr}(H,\mathbb{R})$. Moreover $\pi_j(\mathrm{Epi}(W,V)^H) = 0$ for

$$j \leq \mathrm{Min}(d(A)(w(A) - v(A)) \mid A \in \mathrm{Irr}(H,\mathbb{R}),\ v(A) > 0)). \ \square$$

We now turn over attention to the transversality problem (10.3). Transversality is a local problem and one tries to make a G-map transverse by induction over the orbit bundles. We describe one typical step of this construction. Let H be a maximal isotropy group of SW and look at H-fixed points

10.16 $SW^H \xrightarrow{F^H} (X^H \times V^H)^+ \longleftarrow X^H \times 0.$

One may replace X up to homotopy by a smooth G-manifold and one can assume that F is smooth on the pre-image of a neighbourhood of $X \times 0$. The group $WH = NH/H$ acts freely on SW^H. It is easy to extend the classical transversality theorem to a situation where one maps a manifold with free action. Thus one can assume that F^H is transverse to $X^H \times 0$ in (10.16) by this extended transversality theorem. If one can cover the map F^H by an equivariant NH-epimorphism of the normal bundle $\nu(SW^H,SW) \mid (F^H)^{-1}(X \times 0)$ onto the normal bundle $\nu(X^H \times V^H, X^H \times V)$, then one would have transversality at the points of $(F^H)^{-1}(X^H \times 0)$. The question about mapping the normal bundles requires an NH-map

10.17 $(F^H)^{-1}(X \times 0) \longrightarrow \mathrm{Epi}(W/W^H, V/V^H)$.

This leads to the same type of obstructions as in (10.15). For more information about the transversality problem see PETRIE [1978].

10.18 Example. Let $G = \mathbb{Z}/m$, $m = p_1p_2\cdots p_r$, p_i different odd prime numbers. We look for representation forms X with $\mathrm{Iso}(X) = \{1, \mathbb{Z}/p_1, \ldots, \mathbb{Z}/p_r\}$. Suppose $\mathrm{Dim}\, X(\mathbb{Z}/p_i) = 2a_i$. Let W_i be an irreducible complex G-representation with kernel $\mathbb{Z}/p_i$. It is possible to choose the W_i in such a way that the $\mathrm{res}_{\mathbb{Z}/p_j} W_i$ for $j \neq i$ are all isomorphic. In order to see this write $W_i = \eta^{b_ip_i}$, where η is the standard representation of $\mathbb{Z}/m \subset S^1$ on $\mathbb{C}$. By the Chinese remainder theorem we can determine integers b_i such that

$$b_i \equiv \frac{m}{p_ip_j} \bmod p_j \quad \text{for} \quad j \neq i.$$

Then $\eta^{b_ip_i}$ is as $\mathbb{Z}/p_j$-representation equal to η^{m/p_j} which is independent of i and a faithful representation. Now let $W = \Sigma a_iW_i$ and suppose

10.19 $$X * SU \simeq SW,$$

where U is a free G-representation. Then the conditions (10.11), (10.15) amount to

10.20 $$2a_i \leqq \sum_{j\neq i} 2a_j - \dim_{\mathbb{R}} U.$$

If, e.g., the a_i are all equal to a and $r \geqq 3$, then (10.20) can be satisfied for

$$\dim_{\mathbb{R}} U \leqq 2(r - 2)a.$$

The gap hypothesis leads in this case to the conditions

$$2 \dim X^{\mathbb{Z}/p_i} = 2(2a_i - 1) < \sum_j 2a_j - \dim_{\mathbb{R}} U - 1 = \dim X$$

which is already covered by (10.20). Note that we can satisfy (10.20) in the case $a_i = a$ with $\dim U = 2(r-2)a$ and hence $\dim X = 4a-1$. Since r can be arbitrarily large we obtain representation forms with a strong deviation from linear homotopy type.

It remains to verify the existence of homotopy types X satisfying (10.19). This follows from the results in section 5.

Remark. Let X be a representation form for $G = \mathbb{Z}/pq$, $p \neq q$ without G-fixed points. One has an inclusion of $\mathbb{Z}/q$-free spaces (actually a G-map)

$$X^{\mathbb{Z}/p} \to X \setminus X^{\mathbb{Z}/q}.$$

Since $X \setminus X^{\mathbb{Z}/q}$ is a homology sphere of dimension $\dim X - \dim X^{\mathbb{Z}/q} - 1$ we obtain from Smith theory that $\dim X^{\mathbb{Z}/p} \leq \dim X - \dim X^{\mathbb{Z}/q} - 1$. We see that there cannot exist representation forms with non-linear dimension function for $\mathbb{Z}/pq$. But there do exist representation forms which are not G-homeomorphic to representations. We will see that one can have actions such that the linking number of $X^{\mathbb{Z}/p}$ and $X^{\mathbb{Z}/q}$ in X is different from ± 1. This remark applies to the $\mathbb{Z}/m$-actions of (10.18), when the action is restricted to $\mathbb{Z}/pq$.

10.21 Example. The examples (10.18) had the qualitative property that the only isotropy groups were p-groups (for some prime p). We shall now show that such examples exist for every nilpotent group.

Let $G = G(p_1) \times \ldots \times G(p_r)$ be the direct product of its p_i-Sylow groups $G(p_i)$. Let r_G denote the regular representation of G over $\mathbb{C}$. We consider homotopy representations X which have only isotropy groups in one of the $G(p_i)$ and which have the dimension function of $|G/G(p_i)| r_{G(p_i)}$ as $G(p_i)$-dimension function. The function $\operatorname{Dim} X$ is stably linear since it satisfies the Borel - Smith conditions, see TOM DIECK [1987], III.5.

There exist rational representations U_1 and U_2 such that

10.22 $\quad \operatorname{Dim} X + \operatorname{Dim} SU_1 = \operatorname{Dim} S(r_G) + \operatorname{Dim} SU_2.$

10.23 Lemma. Given U_1 and U_2 such that (10.22) holds. There exists a finite homotopy type X such that $X * SU_1 \simeq S(r_G) * SU_2$.

We assume this lemma. Let $H \subset G$ be a p-group, $p \in \{p_1,\ldots,p_r\}$. The representations SU_1 and SU_2 have the same dimension function as p-groups by construction. We conclude from this fact that they are isomorphic since U_1 and U_2 are rational representations (SERRE [1971]).

For more information about the topic of this section see MADSEN - RAUSSEN [1985].

11. Linking of fixed point sets in representation forms.

We consider representation forms X of a group G such that $Iso(X) = \{1,H,K\}$. We are particularly interested in the linking of the fixed point sets X^H and X^K in X.

Since $gHg^{-1} \in Iso(X)$ there are two cases to consider:

11.1 H is a normal subgroup.

11.2 There exists $g \in G$ such that $gHg^{-1} = K$.
Then $|G/NH| = |G/NK| = 2$. The groups NH and NK of index 2 in G must be normal subgroups. Since H and K are conjugate we have $NH = NK$.

For the relative position of H and K there are again two cases:

11.3 None of the groups is contained in the other.

11.4 With suitable notation, $H \subset K$.
(11.4) implies (11.1). This case can occur for e.g. suitable representation spheres $S(V)$ of $G = \mathbb{Z}/p^3$. Since this case does not lead to linking systems we assume that (10.3) holds.

<u>11.5 Lemma</u>. $H \cap K = 1$ and $X^H \cap X^K = \emptyset$.

<u>Proof</u>. Let $L = H,K$ be the group generated by H and K. The union

$$X^H \cap X^K = X^L = \cup \{X^U | U \supset L,\ U \in Iso(X)\}$$

is the empty union since there are no $U \in Iso(X)$ with $U \supset L$. Let $1 \neq g \in H \cap K$. Then

$$X^g = \cup \{X^U | g \in U,\ U \in Iso\ X\} = X^H \cup X^K$$

is a disjoint union.

If g has prime power order this contradicts Smith theory. □

11.6 Lemma. NH/H, NK/K, H and K are groups with periodic cohomology.

Proof. NH/H acts freely on X^H. By (11.5) K acts freely on X^H. □

11.7 Remark. If X is a smooth representation form, then H acts freely on the fibre of the normal bundle of X^H in X. Thus H and K belong to the smaller class of groups which possess free representations.

Consider the case (11.1). Let $p_H : G \longrightarrow G/H$ and $p_K : G \longrightarrow G/K$ denote the quotient maps. Then $(p_H, p_K) : G \longrightarrow G/H \times G/K$ is injective and

$$\begin{array}{ccc} G & \longrightarrow & G/H \\ \downarrow & & \downarrow \\ G/K & \longrightarrow & G/HK \end{array}$$

is a pullback. In particular G is a subgroup of a product of two periodic groups.

Conversely, let G_1, G_2, and G_3 be periodic groups and

$$\begin{array}{ccc} G & \xrightarrow{i_1} & G_1 \\ {\scriptstyle i_2}\downarrow & & \downarrow{\scriptstyle p_1} \\ G_2 & \xrightarrow{p_2} & G_3 \end{array}$$

a pullback with surjective p_1 and p_2. Then

11.8 Lemma. (i) i_1 and i_2 are surjective.

(ii) $G_j \cong G/H_j$, $H_j := \ker i_j$.

(iii) $G_3 \cong G/H_1H_2$, $H_1 \cap H_2 = \{1\}$.

(iv) $(i_1, i_2) : G \longrightarrow G_1 \times G_2$ is injective. □

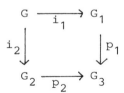

Suppose $\dim X^H + \dim X^K + 1 = \dim X$. Then we have a linking number v of X^H and X^K in X. (We assume X to be orientable and oriented.)

<u>11.9 Proposition</u>. The linking number is prime to $|G|$.

<u>Proof</u>. The inclusion $i : X^H \longrightarrow X \smallsetminus X^K$ is a G-map. If $L \cap H = \{1\}$, this is a map between L-free homology spheres. By Smith theory the degree of i is prime to $|L|$. In particular we can take $L = K$. If p is a prime divisor of $|G|$ but not of $|H||K|$ we can choose $L \cong \mathbb{Z}/p$. □

The linking number is not a homotopy invariant but determines the homotopy type once the equivariant homotopy types of X^H and X^K are fixed. We are going to explain this statement. Let us assume case (11.1) and $\dim X^H \geqq 2 \leqq \dim X^K$.

<u>11.10 Proposition</u>. $X \smallsetminus X^H$ is a generalized homotopy representation and X is G-homotopy equivalent to $X^H * (X \smallsetminus X^H)$.

<u>Proof</u>. Using duality we see that $X \smallsetminus X^H$ has the integral homology of a sphere. Since $\operatorname{codim} X^H \geqq 3$ the space $X \smallsetminus X^H$ is simply connected and hence homotopy equivalent to a sphere. The only nontrivial fixed point set of $X \smallsetminus X^H$ is X^K. Therefore, $X \smallsetminus X^H$ has all fixed point sets homotopy equivalent to a sphere and is thus, by definition, a generalized homotopy representation.

One has (as in Spanier-Whitehead theory) a duality map

$$d : X \longrightarrow X^H * (X \smallsetminus X^H)$$

which is a G-map and a homotopy equivalence on all fixed points sets, hence a G-equivalence. (Recall: d is constructed as follows: Let U be a tubular G-neighbourhood of X^H in X. Let (φ_1, φ_2) be a G-invariant partition of unity subordinate to $(U, X \smallsetminus X^H)$.

Define

$$d' : X \longrightarrow U * (X \setminus X^H), \quad x \longmapsto (\varphi_1(x)x, \dot{\varphi}_2(x)x).$$

Note $X^H \simeq U$.) □

Let $i : X^K \longrightarrow X \setminus X^H$ be the inclusion. Then $id * i : X^H * X^K \longrightarrow X^H * (X \setminus X^H) \simeq X$ has invertible degree function (10.9). Thus we can use $id * i$ to compare the G-homotopy type of X and $X^H * X^K$. Note that the degree function is determined by the linking number $v = \deg i$.

<u>11.11 Proposition</u>. The G-homotopy type of X is determined by the following three data:

(i) K-homotopy type of X^H.

(ii) H-homotopy type of X^K.

(iii) $\pm v \bmod |G|$.

<u>Proof</u>. Suppose X and Y are representation forms with equal data (i)-(iii). We have seen that there exists a G-map $f: X^H * X^K \longrightarrow X$ of total degree v and $\deg f^L = 1$ for $L \neq 1$. Therefore, there exists a G-map $h : X \longrightarrow X^H * X^K$ with total degree satisfying $v \deg h \equiv 1 \bmod |G|$ and $\deg h^L = 1$ for $L \neq 1$. Since $X^H \simeq Y^H$, $X^K \simeq Y^K$ we have a G-map $k : X^H * X^K \longrightarrow Y$ with the same degree function as f. The map kh satisfies $\deg((kh)^L) = 1$ for all L. By the equivariant Hopf theorem there exists a G-homotopy equivalence. □

<u>11.12 Proposition</u>. Let X be a representation form with linking number v. The trivial $\mathbb{Z}G$-module $\mathbb{Z}/v$ has a free resolution $0 \longrightarrow F_1 \longrightarrow F_0 \longrightarrow \mathbb{Z}/v \longrightarrow 0$ with finitely generated free $\mathbb{Z}G$-modules F_i.

<u>Remark</u>. If the $\mathbb{Z}G$-module M is a finite abelian group of order prime to $|G|$, then there exists a resolution $0 \rightarrow P_1 \rightarrow P_2 \rightarrow M \rightarrow 0$ with finitely-generated projective $\mathbb{Z}G$-modules P_i.

Proof of (11.12). Let $f : X^H * X^K \longrightarrow X$ be the map as in the proof of (10.11). Let $C(f)$ denote the mapping cone of f. Then $\tilde{H}_*(C(f)$ has a single non-vanishing group isomorphic to $\mathbb{Z}/v$. Moreover the $C(f)^L$ for $L \neq 1$ are contractible. Let $C(f)_s$ denote the singular set of $C(f)$. Then $C = C(f)/C(f)_s$ is a finite G-complex with free G-action apart from the base point and a single non-vanishing homology groups $\tilde{H}_n(C) \cong \mathbb{Z}/v$. This fact implies by standard homological algebra that $\mathbb{Z}/v$ has a free resolution by finitely generated free $\mathbb{Z}G$-modules of finite length; by the Schanuel lemma and the remark above there is then a resolution of length two as claimed. □

11.13 Example. Let $G = \mathbb{Z}/p \times \mathbb{Z}/p$, p odd. Then $\mathbb{Z}/v$ has a free resolution as in (11.2) if and only if v is a p-th power mod p^2 (v prime to p assumed). Thus for this group not all integers prime to p can occur as a linking number of the fixed point sets.□

11.14 Example. Suppose H and K are cyclic groups. Suppose $G = H \times K$. The fixed point sets X^H(resp. X^K) have the K-(resp. H-)homotopy type of representation spheres SV_H (resp. SV_K). If X would have linear homotopy type, then this homotopy would have to be $S(V_H \oplus V_K) \cong SV_H * SV_K$. Therefore, X has linear homotopy type if and only if the linking number satisfies $v \equiv \pm 1 \bmod |G|$.□

One can show that representation forms with exotic linking numbers exist. We make the following assumptions: Let $G = H_0 \times H_1$. Suppose H_0 and H_1 are periodic groups and let V_i be a free complex representation of H_i, viewed as G-representation, with $\dim_{\mathbb{R}} V_i \geq 6$. Let $v > 0$ be an integer prime to $|G|$ such that $\mathbb{Z}/v$ has a free resolution as in (11.12).

11.15 Theorem. Let $|G|$ be odd. Then there exists a representation form X of G with dimension function of $S(V_0 \oplus V_1)$ and linking number $v(X^H, v^K) = v$. Moreover X can be chosen to be tangentially bordant to the v-fold sum $v\, S(V_0 \oplus V_1) = M$ with its canonical framing $TM \oplus \varepsilon \longrightarrow V_0 \oplus V_1$.

Proof. TOM DIECK - LÖFFLER [1985],[1986]. □

References

Atiyah, M.F. (1967) K-theory. New York - Amsterdam: Benjamin.

Atiyah, M.F. (1968) Bott periodicity and the index of elliptic operators. Quart.J.Math. Oxford(2)19,113-140.

Bredon, G.E. (1972) Introduction to compact transformation groups. New York: Academic Press.

Brieskorn, E. (1966) Beispiele zur Differentialtopologie von Singularitäten. Invent.math.2,1-14.

Bröcker, Th., and tom Dieck, T. (1985) Representations of compact Lie groups. Berlin-Heidelberg-New York: Springer

Cappell, S., and Shaneson, J. (1984) Linking numbers in branched covers. Four-manifold theory, Contemp.Math.35(AMS),165-179.

Cartan, H., and Eilenberg, S. (1956) Homological Algebra.Princeton: Princeton Univ. Press.

tom Dieck, T. (1978) Homotopy equivalent group representations and Picard groups of the Burnside ring and the character ring. Manuscripta math. 26, 179-200.

tom Dieck, T. (1985) The Picard group of the Burnside ring. J. für die reine und angew. Mathematik 361, 174-200.

tom Dieck, T. (1986) Glatte Darstellungsformen I -Verschlingungssysteme- Math. Gott. 55.

tom Dieck, T. (1987) Transformation groups. Berlin - New York: W. de Gruyter.

tom Dieck, T., and Löffler, P. (1985) Verschlingung von Fixpunktmengen in Darstellungsformen. I. Algebraic topology, Proc.Conf., Göttingen 1984. Lect.Notes Math.1172,167-187.

tom Dieck, T., and Löffler, P. (1986) Verschlingungszahlen von Fixpunktmengen in Darstellungsformen. II. Transformation groups, Proc.Conf., Poznań 1985, Lect.Notes Math. 1217, 84-91.

tom Dieck, T., and Löffler, P. (1978) Geometric modules over the Burnside ring. Invent.math. 47, 273-287.

tom Dieck, T., and Petrie, T. (1982) Homotopy representations of finite groups. Publ.math. I.H.E.S. 56, 129-169.

Dold, A. (1963) Partitions of unity in the theory of fibrations. Ann. of Math. 78, 223-255.

Hirzebruch, F., and Mayer, K.H. (1968) O(n)-Mannigfaltigkeiten, exot. Sphären u. Singularitäten. Lect.Notes in Math.57. Berlin - Heidelberg - New York: Springer.

Kervaire, M.A., and Milnor, J. (1963) Groups of homotopy spheres I. Ann.of Math. 77, 504-537.

Laitinen, E. (1986) Unstable homotopy theory of homotopy representations. Transformation groups, Proc. Conf., Poznań 1985, Lect. Notes Math. 1217, 210-248 (1986

Mac Lane, S. (1963) Homology. Berlin-Göttingen-Heidelberg: Springer.

Madsen, I., and Raußen, M. (1985) Smooth and locally linear G-homotopy representations. Algebraic topology, Proc.Conf., Göttingen'84. Lect. Notes Math. 1172, 130-156.

Milnor, J. (1957) Groups which act on S^n without fixed points. Amer. J. Math. 79, 623-630.

Montgomery, D., and Yang, C.T. (1981) Dihedral group actions I. General topology and modern analysis. Conf.Proc., Riverside California 1980,295-307. New York, Academic Press.

Petrie, T. (1971) Free metacyclic group actions on homotopy spheres. Ann. of Math. 94, 108-124.

Petrie, T. (1978a) Pseudoequivalences of G-manifolds. Algebraic and geometric topology, Proc.Conf., Stanford 1976, Proc. of Symposia in Pure Math.32 Part.1,169-210.

Petrie, T. (1979) Three theorems in transformation groups. Lect. Notes in Math. 763, 549-572.

Segal, G.B. (1968) Equivariant K-theory. Publ. Math. Inst. Hautes Études Sci. 34, 129-151.

Serre, J.-P. (1971) Répresentations linéaires des groupes finis. Paris: Hermann 2. éd.

Spanier, E.H. (1966) Algebraic topology. New York: Mc Graw-Hill.

Swan, R.G. (1960) Periodic resolutions for finite groups. Ann. of Math. 72, 267-291.

Swan, R.G. (1960a) The p-period of a finite group. Illinois J. Math. 4, 341-346.

Wall, C.T.C. ((1966) Surgery of non-simply connected manifolds. Ann. of Math. 84, 217-276.

Wall, C.T.C. (1979) Periodic projective resolutions. Proc. London Math. Soc. 39, 509-533-

Whitehead, G.W. (1978) Elements of homotopy theory. New York-Heidelberg-Berlin: Springer.

Wolf, J.A. (1967) Spaces of constant curvature. New York: Mc Graw-Hill.

An Introduction to Calculations in Surgery

Ian Hambleton

Lecture 1.

The purpose of these lectures is to survey some of the methods available for determining surgery obstructions for surgery problems with finite fundamental groups. These methods are mostly algebraic but the algebra is motivated by geometry, so to begin we will describe the geometrical setting for surgery. The sources used in each lecture are given at the end, and the reader should refer to them for proofs and references to the original work.

Suppose that W^{n+1} is a smooth compact manifold with two boundary components M_0 and M_1. Let $f\colon W \to [0,1]$ denote a Morse function, namely a smooth function with $f(M_0) = 0$, $f(M_1) = 1$, non-degenerate critical points and distinct critical values

$$0 < c_1 < c_2 < \dots < c_r < 1.$$

By the Morse lemma, in a neighborhood U of a critical point $p_0 \in W$ with $f(p_0) = c$, there exists a co-ordinate system $x_i = x_i(p)$, $1 \le i \le n+1$, so that

$$f(p) = f(p_0) - x_1^2 - \dots - x_k^2 + x_{k+1}^2 + \dots + x_{n+1}^2$$

for all $p \in U$. The integer k, $0 \le k \le n+1$ is the index of the critical point. If $\varepsilon > 0$ is so small that $W_0 = f^{-1}([c-\varepsilon, c+\varepsilon])$ has no critical points other than p_0, then $M_{c+\varepsilon} = f^{-1}(c+\varepsilon)$ is obtained from $M_{c-\varepsilon}$ by an elementary surgery of type $(k, n-k)$:

$$M_{c+\varepsilon} = (M_{c-\varepsilon} - \varphi(S^{k-1} \times D^{n-k+1})) \cup_\varphi (D^k \times S^{n-k})$$

where $\varphi : S^{k-1} \times D^{n-k+1} \longrightarrow M_{c-\varepsilon}$ is an embedding. The manifold W_0 is diffeomorphic to $(M_{c-\varepsilon} \times I) \cup (D^k \times D^{n-k+1})$ and is usually called the trace of the surgery. This is the basic construction.

The discussion above shows that the equivalence relation cobordism of manifolds is generated by elementary surgeries. To reverse this point of view, and produce a scheme for the classification of manifolds requires a good bookkeeping system for elementary surgeries. First we define, for any space X, the n–dimensional structure set $\mathcal{S}_n(X)$. This is the set of equivalence classes of pairs (M^n, f) where M^n is a closed n–manifold and $f : M \longrightarrow X$ is a homotopy equivalence. Two such pairs (M_0, f_0), (M_1, f_1) are equivalent if there is a diffeomorphism $h: M_0 \longrightarrow M_1$ such that $f_1 \circ h \simeq f_0$ (a useful variation is to assume that two pairs are equivalent if they are h–cobordant). One can now ask for a "computation" of $\mathcal{S}_n(X)$ given X. If we start with X a closed n–manifold, and then $\mathcal{S}_n(X)$ measures the manifolds in the same homotopy type.

A more flexible assumption is that X has the main homotopy properties of a manifold. In more detail, we say that X is a (finite) Poincaré duality space of formal dimension n, if X is a homotopy equivalent to a (finite) CW–complex with cells in dimensions $\leq n$ and has a fundamental class $[X] \in H^t_n(X;\mathbb{Z})$ such that

$$[X] \cap : H^i(X) \longrightarrow H^t_{n-i}(X)$$

is an isomorphism for all $i \geq 0$. Here we are using (co)homology with $\Lambda := \mathbb{Z}[\pi_1 X]$ coefficients. The definition for any (right) Λ–module B is,

$$H^*(X;B) = H(\mathrm{Hom}_\Lambda(C_*(X),B))$$
$$H^t_*(X;B) = H(C_*(X) \otimes_\Lambda B).$$

In order to define the tensor product, B is made into a left Λ–module by the rule $\lambda \cdot b = b\bar{\lambda}$. The anti–automorphism $\lambda \longrightarrow \bar{\lambda}$ on Λ is defined by

$$\sum n_g g \longrightarrow \sum n_g \omega(g) g^{-1}.$$

where $\omega: \pi_1(X) \longrightarrow \{\pm 1\}$ is the homomorphism given by the first Wu class. Loops having class α with $w(\alpha) = 1$ are thought of as orientation–preserving; mostly we will assume that $w \equiv 1$ (the oriented case). Note that for $B = \Lambda$, $H_i(X) = H_i(\tilde{X};\mathbb{Z})$ where $\tilde{X}$ is the universal covering space of X. If X is a manifold, then X is a finite Poincaré complex in the above sense, and ω (according to the Wu formula) is given by the first Stiefel–Whitney class $\omega_1(X)$.

We remark that it is sometimes convenient to assume that X has Poincaré duality only in a range of dimensions. The target spaces for surgery can be adapted to the specific geometric problem. For an extreme example, it is sometimes convenient to regard a map $X \longrightarrow K(\pi,1)$ as a surgery problem.

A Poincaré space X^n resembles a manifold in another important way. Let $X \longrightarrow \mathbb{R}^{n+k}$ be an embedding (k is large) and N a regular neighborhood. Then it turns out that the composite $i: \partial N \longrightarrow N \xrightarrow{\simeq} X$ is (up to homotopy) a spherical fibration, with each fibre homotopy equivalent to S^{k-1}. If k is sufficiently large, this fibration ν_X is unique up to fibre homotopy equivalence and is called the Spivak normal fibre space of X. By construction, the collapse map

$$c : S^{n+k} \longrightarrow \mathbb{R}^{n+k}/\mathbb{R}^{n+k} - N = T(\nu)$$

together with the Thom isomorphism Φ induces a degree 1 map

$$H_{n+k}(S^{n+k};\mathbb{Z}) \xrightarrow{c_*} H_{n+k}(T(\nu);\mathbb{Z}) \underset{\approx}{\xleftarrow{\Phi}} H^t_n(X;\mathbb{Z})$$

taking a generator $[S^{n+k}]$ onto $[X]$. Conversely, the Spivak normal fibre space is characterized, up to stable fibre homotopy equivalence, as a spherical fibration ν over X such that $\pi_{n+k}(T(\nu))$ contains a map of degree 1.

We now define a degree 1 normal map with target (X,ω). This consists of a degree 1 map $f: M^n \to X$ where M is a closed n–manifold, together with a bundle map $b: \nu_M \to \xi$ covering f, for some vector bundle ξ over X. Alternatively, one can suppose that $\tau_M \oplus f^*(\xi)$ has a stable trivialization. Two normal maps (M_i,f_i,b_i), i=0,1 are normally cobordant if there is a cobordism W^{n+1} from M_0 to M_1 and maps

$$F:W \to X\times I, \quad B: \nu_N \to \xi \oplus 1$$

extending (f_i,b_i). The set of normal maps with target (X,ω) is denoted $T(X,\omega)$. Note that from the discussion above, each bundle ξ occurring in a degree 1 normal map must be fibre homotopy equivalent to ν_X (such a ξ is called a vector bundle reduction of ν_X). The elements of $T(X,\omega)$ are in bijection with the set of all elements of degree 1 in $\pi_{n+k}(T(\xi))$ as ξ varies over all vector bundle reductions of ν_X for k large.

A primary obstruction for the existence of any manifold homotopy equivalent to X is therefore the existence of some reduction of the spherical fibration ν_X to a vector bundle. For arbitrary Poincaré complexes X reductions need not exist, but this turns out to be a homotopy–theoretic problem. Assuming that $T(X,\omega)$ is non–empty, we seek a procedure for determining when a normal map is normally cobordant to a homotopy equivalence.

We first notice that the set $T(X,\omega)$ is a good book–keeping device. If $f: M \to X$ is a degree 1 map, the main observation is that the diagram

$$\begin{array}{ccc} H^{n-i}(M) & \xleftarrow{f^*} & H^{n-i}(X) \\ \downarrow \cap[M] & & \downarrow \cap[X] \\ H_i^t(M) & \xrightarrow{f_*} & H_i^t(X) \end{array}$$

commutes. Therefore, in each dimension, f_* is split surjective and f^* is split injective. Let $K_i(f)$, (resp. $K^i(f)$) denote the i–dimensional kernel (resp. cokernel) of f_* (resp. f^*). Then

$[M]\cap$ induces an isomorphism of $K^{n-i}(f)$ onto $K_i(f)$ for all $i \geq 0$. Now f is a homotopy equivalence if and only if it induces an isomorphism on π_1 and $K_i(f) = 0$ for all $i \geq 0$.

Furthermore, if $b: \nu_M \to \xi$ is a bundle map covering f and

$$\phi : S^i \to M$$

is an embedding of a sphere in M with $f \circ \phi \simeq *$, then $\phi^* \nu_M = \phi^* f^* (\xi)$ is a trivial bundle. Since the tangent bundle of a sphere is trivial after stabilizing once, we see that $\phi(S^i)$ has trivial normal bundle in M if $i < [n/2]$. Therefore, starting with a degree 1 normal map, we can simplify it by elementary surgeries, to obtain:

Proposition. A degree 1 normal map $(f,b): M^n \to X$ is normally cobordant to an $[n/2]$–connected normal map.

Proof. By elementary surgeries on 0 and 1 spheres we can assume that f induces an isomorphism on π_0 and π_1. By induction we assume that f is i–connected for $i+1 \leq [n/2]$. Then $\pi_{i+1}(f) \cong K_i(f)$ and any element is represented by an embedded i–sphere with trivial normal bundle. We perform an elementary surgery on this class and extend f over the trace of the surgery. If we use the normal bundle trivialization arising from an extension of $f \circ \phi$ over D^{i+1}, it can be shown that the bundle map b also extends over the trace of the surgery. To prove this one can use the classification of immersions (as in Wall, p.10), or follow the explicit argument of Kervaire–Milnor, pp.521–522.

Remark. When we do surgery on an i–sphere, the homology class in $K_i(f)$ carried by this sphere is eliminated, but a dual class in dimension $(n-i-1)$ is introduced. If $i < [n/2]$ the new class is in a dimension $\geq [n/2]$, so progress can be made easily. It remains to discuss the middle dimensions. Note that if $n = 2k$ and we do surgery on a trivial $S^{k-1} \times D^{k+1}$ (i.e. contained in a 2k–disk in M), the result is to replace M by $M \# S^k \times S^k$ and $\Lambda \oplus \Lambda$ is added to $K_k(f)$. Similarly, if $n = 2k+1$ and we surger $S^k \times D^{k+1} \subset D^{2k+1}$, we get $M \# S^k \times S^{k+1}$ and

Λ is added to $K_k(f)$ and $K_{k+1}(f)$.

Sources

M.A.Kervaire and J. Milnor,
"Groups of homotopy spheres, I", Ann. of Math. 77 (1963), 504–537.
J.Milnor,
"A procedure for killing the homotopy groups of differentiable manifolds", A.M.S. Symposia in Pure Math. III(1961),39–55.
J.Milnor,
Morse Theory, Ann. of Math. Studies 51, Princeton University Press, 1961.
M.Spivak,
"Spaces satisfying Poincaré duality", Topology 6 (1967), 77–102
R.Thom,
Quelques propriétés globales des variétés différentiables",Comm. Math. Helv. 28 (1954), 17–86.
C.T.C.Wall,
Surgery on Compact Manifolds: Chap.1&2, Academic Press, 1970..

Lecture 2.

In the first lecture we saw that any degree 1 normal map $f: M^n \to X$ could be assumed [n/2]–connected. If $n=2k$, it is no longer true that every class in $K_k(f)$ is represented by an embedded sphere with trivial normal bundle. Since $L = K_k(f) = \pi_{k+1}(f)$ is the single non–trivial homology group of the chain complex $C_*(f)$ of the mapping cone, it follows that L is a stably–free finitely generated Λ–module. By surgery on some trivial (k–1)–spheres, we may assume L is a free Λ–module. So is $K^k(f) \cong \mathrm{Hom}_\Lambda(K_k(f),\Lambda)$, where the isomorphism is given by Poincaré duality. This gives a pairing

$$\lambda : L \times L \to \Lambda$$

induced by intersection numbers, which will now be described more explicitly.

According to a theorem of Haefliger, regular homotopy classes of immersions $\phi: S^k \to M^{2k}$ correspond bijectively (by the tangent map) to stable homotopy classes of stable bundle monomorphisms $\tau_{S^k} \to \phi^* \tau_M$. We can therefore represent elements of $K_k(f)$ by immersions equipped with a path in M joining a fixed base point $x_0 \in M$ to $\phi(p_0)$, where

$p_0 \in S^k$ is a basepoint. These immersions may be chosen so that the normal bundle is trivial, and this specifies the regular homotopy class uniquely. Note that $\pi_1(M,x_0)$ acts on such an immersed sphere by composing the path with a loop at x_0.

Let S_1 and S_2 be two immersed k–spheres in M, meeting transversely in a finite set of points $\{P\}$. To each point P we assign a fundamental group element g_P and an orientation $\varepsilon_P = \pm 1$. The Λ–valued intersection form is defined by

$$\lambda(S_1,S_2) = \sum_P \varepsilon_P g_P.$$

This is related to the ordinary intersection form $\lambda_0\colon L \times L \longrightarrow \mathbb{Z}$ by the formula

$$\lambda(x,y) = \sum_{g \in \pi_1} \lambda_0(x,yg^{-1})g.$$

The same procedure can be used to define the self–intersection of an immersed sphere S_1 (in general position, so that it has a finite set of transverse intersections where two branches meet). At each intersection point P, after an order of the branches is chosen, the quantities ε_P and g_P are defined as before. If the order is interchanged, $\varepsilon_P g_P$ becomes $(-1)^k \omega(g_P)\varepsilon_P g_P^{-1} = (-1)^k \varepsilon_P \bar{g}_P$ (using the notation introduced earlier for the anti–involution). Therefore, the self–intersection defines a map

$$\mu : L \longrightarrow \Lambda / \{\nu - (-1)^k \bar{\nu} : \nu \in \Lambda\}.$$

Notice that $\lambda(x,x)$ is computed from the mutual intersections of two immersed spheres representing the class x. If we take S_1' as a cross–section of a tubular neighbourhood of S_1, then each self–intersection point P of S_1 gives two intersection points P' and P'' between S_1 and S_1'. The properties of the quadratic form (L,λ,μ) are summarized in,

Theorem.

(i) For $x \in L$ fixed, $y \longrightarrow \lambda(x,y)$ is a Λ–homomorphism $L \longrightarrow \Lambda$

(ii) $\lambda(y,x) = (-1)^k\overline{\lambda(x,y)}$, for $x,y \in L$.

(iii) $\lambda(x,x) = \mu(x) + (-1)^k\overline{\mu(x)}$, for $x \in L$.

(iv) $\mu(x+y) - \mu(x)) - \mu(y) = \lambda(x,y)$, for $x,y \in L$.

(v) $\mu(xa) = \bar{a}\mu(x)a$, for $x \in L$, $a \in \Lambda$.

(vi) If $k \geq 3$, x is represented by an embedding with trivial normal bundle if and only if $\mu(x) = 0$.

We remark that part (vi) involves the "Whitney trick" which fails for smooth or PL immersions of 2–spheres in a four–dimensional manifold. Recently M.Freedman proved that surgery works for topological four–manifolds with "sufficiently nice" (including finite) fundamental groups.

To relate this algebra to the problem of eliminating $K_k(f)$, there are just two geometric observations to be made.

(i) If $(f,b):M \longrightarrow X$ is normally cobordant to a homotopy equivalence, then (L,λ,μ) contains a free–direct summand L_0 such that $\lambda|L_0{\times}L_0 \equiv 0$ and $\mu(L_0) \equiv 0$. This is called a subkernel. An easy algebraic argument implies that a quadratic form contains a subkernel if and only if it is isomorphic to an orthogonal direct sum of hyperbolic planes (these are free Λ–modules of rank 2 with base $\langle x,y \rangle$, $\mu(x) = \mu(y) = 0$ and $\lambda(x,y) = 1$).

(ii) A hyperbolic plane can be removed from (L,λ,μ) by surgery on one of the basis elements if $k \geq 3$. The picture to keep in mind here is the thickening in M (with trivial normal bundles) of two embedded k–spheres that intersect transversely in one point. This thickening is a compact manifold diffeomorphic to $S^k \times S^k - D^{2k}$ with boundary S^{2k-1}. The effect of the surgery is to remove the interior of the thickening and repace it with D^{2k}.

These points motivate the definition of the even–dimensional surgery obstruction group $L_{2k}(\mathbb{Z}[\pi_1 X],\omega)$: it is the stable isomorphism classes of $(-1)^k$–quadratic forms (L,λ,μ) on free Λ–modules L, modulo hyperbolic forms. Here "stable isomorphism" means that the forms become isomorphic after adding hyperbolics.

The odd–dimensional case leads to a more complicated situation. Let $(f,b)\colon M^{2k+1} \to X$ be a degree 1 normal map with $K_i(f) = 0$ for $i < k$. Choose a set of embeddings $\phi_j\colon S^k \times D^{k+1} \to M$ (each joined by a path to the base–point) such that $\{\phi_j \mid S^k{\times}0\}$ is a set of generators for $K_k(f)$ as a Λ–module. These may be assumed to have disjoint images in M, so let U be the union of the images and $M_0 = M - U$. We assume further that $f(U) = * \in X$, and $X = X_0 \cup D^{2k+1}$ where $(X_0,\partial X_0)$ is a finite Poincaré pair. We can then obtain a map of triads

$$f : (M,M_0,U) \to (X,X_0,D^{2k+1}),$$

leading to the diagram (see [Wall,Chap. 6]):

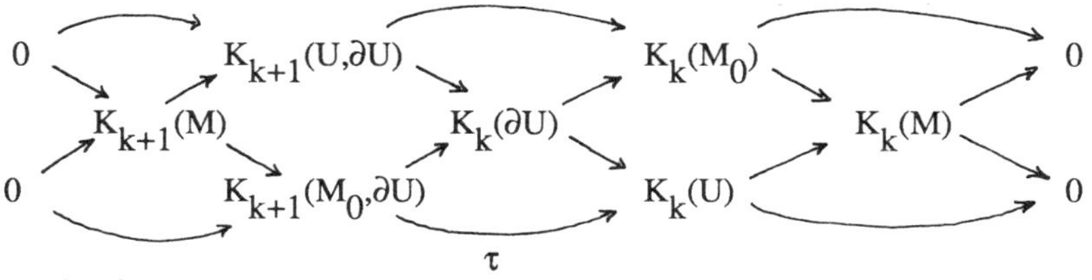

Now $\partial U \approx \#(S^k{\times}S^k)_i$, so $K_k(\partial U)$ is a hyperbolic form with two standard subkernels $K_{k+1}(U,\partial U)$ and $K_k(U)$. Furthermore $K_{k+1}(M_0,\partial U)$ is <u>also</u> a subkernel in $K_k(\partial U)$.

From the diagram above, $K_k(M)$ and $K_{k+1}(M)$ are trivial if and only if the map τ, which depends on the choice of embeddings $\{\phi_i\}$, is an isomorphism. Two subkernels L, L' in a hyperbolic form H are said to be complementary if $H \cong L \oplus L'$ as quadratic forms. The main observation is that τ is an isomorphism if and only if $K_{k+1}(M_0,\partial U)$ is a complementary subkernel to $K_{k+1}(U,\partial U)$ for some choice of the $\{\phi_i\}$.

The discussion so far suggests that the relevant data is $(H(\Lambda^r),L_0,L_1)$ where $H(\Lambda^r)$ is the hyperbolic form $(\Lambda^r \oplus \Lambda^t, \begin{pmatrix} 0 & 0 \\ 1 & 0 \end{pmatrix})$ and L_0,L_1 are two subkernels. This is correct and the precise definitions are due to Ranicki (following earlier work of Mischenko). For our purposes, the original definition of Wall for $L_{2k+1}(\mathbb{Z}[\pi_1 X],\omega)$ is better. It rests on an algebraic fact:

<u>Lemma</u>. If L_0,L_1 are subkernels in a quadratic form (L,λ,μ), then any Λ–isomorphism $\theta : L_0 \to L_1$ extends to an isometry of (L,λ,μ).

Let $SU_r(\Lambda)$ denote the group of isometries of the standard hyperbolic form $H(\Lambda^r)$, and $TU_r(\Lambda)$ the subgroup leaving the subkernel $\Lambda^r \oplus 0$ invariant. A detailed analysis of the construction above, shows that there is a well–defined invariant after allowing for

(i) stabilization: $SU_r(\Lambda) \subset SU_{r+1}(\Lambda) \subset \ldots \subset SU(\Lambda)$

(ii) the action of $TU_r(\Lambda) \subset TU_{r+1}(\Lambda) \subset \ldots \subset TU(\Lambda)$, and

(iii) interchanging $\Lambda^r \oplus 0$ and $0 \oplus \Lambda^r$.

Let $\sigma = \begin{pmatrix} 0 & 1 \\ (-1)^k & 0 \end{pmatrix} \in SU_1(\Lambda)$ and $RU(\Lambda)$ be the subgroup of $SU(\Lambda)$ generated by σ and $TU(\Lambda)$. Then surgery to a homotopy equivalence is possible, if and only if our automorphism (relating $K_{k+1}(U,\partial U)$ to $K_{k+1}(M_0,\partial U)$) is equivalent modulo to $\sigma \oplus \sigma \oplus \ldots \oplus \sigma$ (the automorphism in (iii) above) under the 2–sided action of $RU(\Lambda)$. Wall finally proves (with the aid of a remarkable identity) that $RU(\Lambda) \supset [SU(\Lambda),SU(\Lambda)]$ and so

$$L_{2k+1}(\mathbb{Z}[\pi_1 X],\omega) = SU(\Lambda)/RU(\Lambda)$$

is an abelian group.

The main outcome of this analysis is:

<u>**Theorem**</u>. If X^n is a finite Poincaré complex and $n \geq 5$, there is an exact sequence (of pointed sets)

$$\mathscr{S}_n(X) \xrightarrow{\eta} T(X,\omega) \xrightarrow{\lambda} L_n(\mathbb{Z}[\pi_1 X],\omega).$$

Wall also proves that $L_n(\mathbb{Z}[\pi_1 X],\omega) \cong L_{n+4}(\mathbb{Z}[\pi_1 X],\omega)$ and that the surgery exact sequence can be extended indefinitely to the left. In the further development of geometric surgery, one studies the kernel of η, the relation of $T(X,\omega)$ to classifying spaces for spherical fibrations, and the "assembly map" description of the surgery obstruction map λ.

One variation of the whole setup which is important for the applications is to take account of Whitehead torsion. The definition for $\mathscr{S}_n(X)$ is given in terms of homotopy equivalences $f: M \longrightarrow X$. Since a homotopy equivalence has a torsion $\tau(f) \in Wh(\mathbb{Z}[\pi_1 X])$, we could define $\mathscr{S}_n^{\tilde{U}}(X)$ for subgroups $\tilde{U} \subseteq Wh(\mathbb{Z}[\pi_1 X])$ by requiring that all torsions lie in U. Notice that Poincaré duality imposes the condition $\tau(f) = (-1)^n \overline{\tau(f)}$ so it is natural to suppose that $\tilde{U}$ is an involution–invariant subgroup. If two homotopy equivalences f_0, f_1 are normally cobordant, then $\tau(f_0) - \tau(f_1) = v + (-1)^n \bar{v}$, for some $v \in Wh(\mathbb{Z}[\pi_1 X])$.

The definition of the surgery obstruction group must then be modified by choosing bases for our free modules, and requiring that any isomorphisms which occur have torsions in $\tilde{U}$. The special choices $\tilde{U} = \{0\}$ and $\tilde{U} = Wh(\mathbb{Z}\pi)$ are denoted L^s and L^h respectively. If $\tilde{U} \subseteq \tilde{V}$ are involution–invariant subgroups of $Wh(\mathbb{Z}[\pi])$ then there is a long exact sequence

$$\ldots \longrightarrow H^{n+1}(\mathbb{Z}/2;\tilde{V}/\tilde{U}) \longrightarrow L_n^{\tilde{U}}(\mathbb{Z}\pi,\omega) \longrightarrow L_n^{\tilde{V}}(\mathbb{Z}\pi,\omega) \longrightarrow H^n(\mathbb{Z}/2;\tilde{V}/\tilde{U}) \longrightarrow \ldots$$

At this point in the development of the theory (1967), the surgery obstruction groups were very little understood. Kervaire–Milnor had shown that $L_n(\mathbb{Z}) = \mathbb{Z}, 0, \mathbb{Z}/2, 0$ for $n \equiv 0,1,2$ and 3 (mod 4) but the method did not easily generalize to other fundamental groups. Quadratic forms and unitary groups had been extensively studied by algebraists, but most of this work assumed that the underlying ring was a field, and from their point of view the integral group ring was not a natural object. Moreover, certain operations, such as change of rings, which were natural algebraically had no geometric analogue, so that it wasn't clear that any purely algebraic calculation could give usable geometric information. What was needed was a complete algebraic version of the theory, and this was supplied by Ranicki, based on the work of Wall and Mischenko.

Sources

C.T.C. Wall, Surgery on Compact Manifolds: Chap.5,6 & 9.

J.A.Lees, "The surgery obstruction groups of C.T.C.Wall", Adv. in Math. 11 (1973), 113–156.

Lecture 3.

The algebraic theory of surgery starts from the notion of a symmetric Poincaré complex (see [Ranicki]). This is a chain complex (not a space !) of finitely–generated projective modules over a ring A with involution $\varepsilon : A \to A$,

$$C : C_n \xrightarrow{d} C_{n-1} \to \dots \to C_1 \xrightarrow{d} C_0,$$

together with a collection of A–module maps

$$\varphi_s : C^{n-r+s} \longrightarrow C_r \quad (s\geq 0)$$

such that

$$d\varphi_s + (-1)^r \varphi_s d^* + (-1)^{n+s-1}(\varphi_{s-1} + (-1)^s T\varphi_{s-1}) = 0$$

and such that the chain map

$$\varphi_0 : C^{n-*} \longrightarrow C_*$$

is a chain equivalence. Here C^{n-*} is the dual complex (shifted by r) and T is the duality involution

$$T : \mathrm{Hom}_A(C^p,C_q) \longrightarrow \mathrm{Hom}_A(C^q,C_p)$$
$$\varphi \longrightarrow (-1)^{pq}\,\varphi^*.$$

The map φ_0 induces the Poincaré duality isomorphisms $H^{n-r}(C) \longrightarrow H_r(C)$, φ_1 is a chain homotopy between φ_0 and $T\varphi_0$, and so on.

If $(f,b)\colon M \longrightarrow X$ is a degree 1 normal map, then the kernel complex $C(f)$ has the structure of an symmetric Poincaré complex. Furthermore, the bundle map b gives in a natural way a quadratic refinement of this structure (or "quadratic Poincaré complex") which determines the surgery obstruction.

One of the main results of the algebraic theory is the description of $L_n(A,\varepsilon)$ as the cobordism group of n–dimensional quadratic Poincaré complexes of free A–modules. This makes sense for any ring A with involution, or even for the more general notion of a ring with antistructure. There is no difficulty in replacing projective A–module chain complexes by free chain complexes in the definition, but we apparently lose the possibility of Whitehead torsion variant L–groups since "Wh(A)" has no natural meaning. However if $\tilde{U} \subseteq \tilde{K}_1(A) = K_1(A)/\{\pm 1\}$ is an involution–invariant subgroup, the groups $L_*^{\tilde{U}}(A,\varepsilon)$ are defined as the cobordism groups of complexes with $\tau(\varphi_0) \in \tilde{U}$. Then if $A = \mathbb{Z}\pi$ and $\tilde{U} = \{\pm\pi^{ab}\}$,

$$L_n^s(\mathbb{Z}\pi) = L_n^{\tilde{U}}(A)$$

since $Wh(\mathbb{Z}\pi) = K_1(\mathbb{Z}\pi)/\{\pm\pi^{ab}\}$.

Notice that $K_1(A{\times}B) = K_1(A) \times K_1(B)$ for any two rings A,B but the same is not true for $\tilde{K}_1(A{\times}B)$. If we add to our chain complexes the requirement that the Euler characteristic $\chi(C) = 0$, then we can define variant L–groups $L_n^U(A,\varepsilon)$ based on involution–invariant subgroups $U \subseteq K_1(A)$. The extreme cases $U = \{0\}$ and $U = K_1(A)$ are denoted L^S and L^K respectively (see "Round L–theory"). These L–groups are well–behaved under products and Morita equivalence.

They are related to the previous groups by an exact sequence,

$$0 \to L^U_{2k}(A,\varepsilon) \to L^{\tilde{U}}_{2k}(A,\varepsilon) \to \mathbb{Z}/2 \to L^U_{2k-1}(A,\varepsilon) \to L^{\tilde{U}}_{2k-1}(A,\varepsilon) \to 0$$

When $A = \mathbb{Z}\pi$ and $U = K_1(A)$, then $L^K_{2k}(\mathbb{Z}\pi) \cong L^h_{2k}(\mathbb{Z}\pi)$ and

$$L^h_{2k+1}(\mathbb{Z}\pi) = L^K_{2k+1}(\mathbb{Z}\pi)/< \begin{pmatrix} 0 & 1 \\ (-1)^k & 0 \end{pmatrix} >.$$

We can alter our original definition of L^h_n and define L^K_n using forms of even rank if $n = 2k$; let $L^K_{2k+1}(\mathbb{Z}\pi) = SU(\Lambda)/TU(\Lambda)$.

The cobordism description provides a uniform way to derive exact sequences, which can then be used for calculations. For example, if $A \to B$ is a map of rings with involution, there is a long exact sequence

$$\ldots \to L_n(A) \to L_n(B) \to L_n(A{\to}B) \to L_{n-1}(A) \to \ldots$$

The most important of these is the "Main Exact Sequence" of Wall. Here we wish to compare $\mathbb{Z}\pi$ to $\mathbb{Q}\pi$, $\hat{\mathbb{Z}}_p\pi$ and $\hat{\mathbb{Q}}_p\pi$. Let $\hat{\mathbb{Z}} = \prod \hat{\mathbb{Z}}_p$ be the profinite completion of the integers and $\hat{\mathbb{Q}}$ is the ring of finite adeles. Note that $\hat{\mathbb{Q}} \subseteq \prod \hat{\mathbb{Q}}_p$ is the subgroup of elements (u_p) such that $u_p \in \hat{\mathbb{Z}}_p$ for all but finitely many primes p.

The square of rings

$$\begin{array}{ccc} \mathbb{Z} & \longrightarrow & \mathbb{Q} \\ \downarrow & & \downarrow \\ \hat{\mathbb{Z}} & \longrightarrow & \hat{\mathbb{Q}} \end{array}$$

satisfies an approximation condition ("E–surjectivity" due to H.Bass), leading to a long exact sequence in K–theory. For certain choices of Whitehead torsion decoration, Wall also obtained a long exact sequence in L–theory.

<u>Theorem 3.1</u> Let π be a finite group and $X = \ker(K_1(\mathbb{Z}\pi) \longrightarrow K_1(\mathbb{Q}\pi))$. Then there is a long exact sequence

$$\ldots \longrightarrow L^S_{n+1}(\hat{\mathbb{Q}}\pi) \longrightarrow L^X_n(\mathbb{Z}\pi) \longrightarrow L^{\hat{X}}_n(\hat{\mathbb{Z}}\pi) \oplus L^S_n(\mathbb{Q}\pi) \longrightarrow L^S_n(\hat{\mathbb{Q}}\pi) \ldots .$$

Here X is the subgroup of $K_1(\mathbb{Z}\pi)$, usually denoted $SK_1(\mathbb{Z}\pi)$, and $\hat{X}$ is its image in $K_1(\hat{\mathbb{Z}}\pi)$.

For geometric surgery problems, we must have the freedom to change our Λ–bases for $C_i(f)$ by elements $g \in \pi_1$. This means that the smallest geometrically relevant torsion decoration containing X is

$$Y = SK_1(\mathbb{Z}\pi) \oplus \{\pm\pi^{ab}\} \subseteq K_1(\mathbb{Z}\pi).$$

Then there are natural maps,

$$L^s_n(\mathbb{Z}\pi) \longrightarrow L^{\tilde{Y}}_n(\mathbb{Z}\pi) \longrightarrow L^h_n(\mathbb{Z}\pi),$$

so that $L^{\tilde{Y}}_n(\mathbb{Z}\pi)$ is "intermediate", between the two L–groups of most geometric significance.

It is worth remarking that the L–groups $L^p_n(\mathbb{Z}\pi)$ based on <u>projective</u> Λ–module chain complexes also have some geometric use. In fact, if $(f,b)\colon M^n \longrightarrow X$ is a degree 1 normal map and X is a finitely dominated (but not necessarily finite) Poincaré duality space, then a surgery obstruction $\lambda(f,b)$ is defined in $L^p_n(\mathbb{Z}[\pi_1 X])$. Moreover when $n \geq 5$, $\lambda(f,b) = 0$ if and only if the product normal map

$$(f,b) \times 1 : M \times S^1 \longrightarrow X \times S^1$$

is normally cobordant to a homotopy equivalence. In addition, the projective L–groups (and their generalizations) are the natural obstruction groups for surgery on non–compact manifolds. The version of this setting which incorporates bounded or controlled surgery problems has been particularly useful (see F.Quinn on "Ends of maps" and Farrell–Hsiang, Farrell–Jones on the Novikov conjecture).

The projective L–groups can also be studied by an arithmetic sequence. If $L_n^P(\mathbb{Z}\pi)$ denotes the L–groups with the added condition $\chi = 0$, then

Theorem 3.2 Let π be a finite group. Then there is an exact squence

$$\dots \longrightarrow L_{n+1}^K(\hat{\mathbb{Q}}\pi) \longrightarrow L_n^P(\mathbb{Z}\pi) \longrightarrow L_n^K(\hat{\mathbb{Z}}\pi) \oplus L_n^K(\mathbb{Q}\pi) \longrightarrow L_n^K(\hat{\mathbb{Q}}\pi) \longrightarrow \dots$$

The exact sequences (3.1) and (3.2) relate the computation of surgery obstruction groups to the L–theory of rings with much better algebraic properties. For example, $\mathbb{Q}\pi = \prod M_{n_i}(D_i)$ where the D_i are skew fields (Wedderburn's theorem) and

$$L_n^K(\mathbb{Q}\pi) = \oplus L_n^K(D_i, \varepsilon_i), \tag{3.3}$$

by invariance under products and Morita equivalence. The terms $L_n^K(D_i, \varepsilon_i)$ must be interpreted with some care: our involution – on $\mathbb{Q}\pi$, induces an involution on the centre of each invariant factor $A_i = M_{n_i}(D_i)$, however in the transition from forms over A_i to forms over D_i a change of symmetry can occur. Nevertheless the formula (3.3) suggests that we should use the rational representation theory of π in a systematic way to organize and simplify the calculation.

The basic building blocks for character theory are the p–hyperelementary groups: extensions

$$1 \longrightarrow C \longrightarrow G \longrightarrow P \longrightarrow 1$$

where C is cyclic of order prime to p and P is a p–group.

Theorem (Dress Induction). Let π be a finite group and $U \subseteq K_1(\mathbb{Z}\pi)$ an involution–invariant subgroup. Then $L_n^U(\mathbb{Z}\pi)$ can be computed in terms of $\{L_n^U(\mathbb{Z}G) : G \subseteq \pi$ is 2–hyperelementary$\}$.

This result means in particular that the sum of all the restricton maps $L_n^U(\mathbb{Z}\pi) \to L_n^U(\mathbb{Z}G)$ to the 2–hyperelementary subgroups is an injection. Therefore to decide whether a surgery obstruction is zero it is sufficient to restrict to these groups. Notice that for a normal map, restriction to a proper subgroup is given geometrically by taking a finite covering of the normal map.

Even with the help of character theory, the group $L_n^K(\mathbb{Q}\pi)$ is not easy to study. For example, $L_0^K(\mathbb{Q})$ is not finitely–generated! A classical way of organizing the calculation is the "local–global" comparison or "Hasse principle". This can be incorporated into our formulation by setting

$$CL_n^U(\mathbb{Q}\pi) = L_n^U(\mathbb{Q}\pi \longrightarrow \hat{\mathbb{Q}}\pi \oplus \mathbb{R}\pi) \tag{3.4}$$

for $U \subseteq K_1(\mathbb{Q}\pi)$, and rewriting (3.1),(3.2) for example as

$$\begin{gathered} \ldots \to CL_{n+1}^S(\mathbb{Q}\pi) \to L_n^X(\mathbb{Z}\pi) \to L_n^{\hat{X}}(\hat{\mathbb{Z}}\pi) \oplus L_n^S(\mathbb{R}\pi) \to CL_n^S(\mathbb{Q}\pi) \ldots \\ \ldots \to CL_{n+1}^K(\mathbb{Q}\pi) \to L_n^P(\mathbb{Z}\pi) \to L_n^K(\hat{\mathbb{Z}}\pi) \oplus L_n^K(\mathbb{R}\pi) \to CL_n^K(\mathbb{Q}\pi) \ldots \end{gathered} \tag{3.5}$$

The computation of the $CL_n^U(D)$ for D a division algebra (with involution) is the deepest part of the theory, and involves methods from Galois cohomology (see Kneser's Tata Institute notes). One of the most striking results is that, when the involution is non–trivial on the centre of D, the groups $CL_n^S(D) = 0$ for all n.

Let us consider now the other terms in (3.5). For $L_n^S(\mathbb{R}\pi)$ or $L_n^K(\mathbb{R}\pi)$ we have an immediate expression (via character theory and Morita equivalence) in terms of the most classical calculations in quadratic forms, namely forms over $\mathbb{R}$, $\mathbb{C}$ and the quaternions H. For these cases, the signature, discriminant (and Pfaffian for L^S) give a complete list of invariants. For later use we note that $L^S_{2k+1} = 0$ for an involution–invariant algebra with centre $(\mathbb{C}, c)$.

The term $L^K_n(\hat{\mathbb{Z}}_p\pi)$ also reduces to quadratic forms over fields, since the L^K–groups have the property that

$$L^K_n(\hat{\mathbb{Z}}_p\pi) = L^K_n(\hat{\mathbb{Z}}_p\pi/J_p\pi)$$

where $J_p\pi \subseteq \hat{\mathbb{Z}}_p\pi$ is the Jacobson radical. The quotient ring is finite and semi–simple (a full matrix ring over a finite field), so we reduce via Morita equivalence to the L^K–groups of finite fields. In odd characteristic, the discriminant (and Pfaffian for L^S) are sufficient invariants; in characteristic 2 we must add in the Arf invariant. We remark that for finite fields with non–trivial involution the L^K–groups are zero in characteristic 2 and the L^S–groups are all zero.

The corresponding term $L^X_n(\hat{\mathbb{Z}}_p\pi)$ in (3.1) is also easy when $p \neq 2$. For p odd,

$$L^X_n(\hat{\mathbb{Z}}_p\pi) \equiv L^S_n(\hat{\mathbb{Z}}_p\pi) \xrightarrow{\approx} L^S_n(\hat{\mathbb{Z}}_p\pi/J_p\pi)$$

and we have L^S–groups of finite fields. If $p = 2$, there is an exact sequence

$$\text{(3.6)} \qquad \cdots \longrightarrow H^{n+1}(K_1(\hat{\mathbb{Z}}_2\pi)/X) \longrightarrow L^X_n(\hat{\mathbb{Z}}_2\pi) \longrightarrow L^K_n(\hat{\mathbb{Z}}_2\pi) \longrightarrow \cdots$$

so the new difficulty is the left–hand term. We will return to this point later.

Even if we completely understand the terms $L^K_i(\hat{\mathbb{Z}}\pi)$ or $L^X_i(\hat{\mathbb{Z}}\pi)$, a problem still remains. If $p \mid |\pi|$, the map

$$(3.7) \qquad L_n^K(\hat{\mathbb{Z}}_p\pi) \longrightarrow L_n^K(\hat{\mathbb{Q}}_p\pi)$$

in (3.5) is badly behaved, since $\hat{\mathbb{Q}}_p\pi$ splits into more factors than $\hat{\mathbb{Z}}_p\pi$ and the image of (3.7) spreads over these factors in a complicated way. To control this problem, we introduce another improvement in the arithmetic sequences. Let $\pi = \mathbb{Z}/m \rtimes \sigma$ be a 2–hyperelementary group, where m is odd and σ is a 2–group. For each $d \mid m$, let

$$R(d) = \mathbb{Z}[\zeta_d]^t\sigma$$

and $S(d) = R(d) \otimes \mathbb{Q}$, $T(d) = R(d) \otimes \mathbb{R}$.

__Theorem 3.8__ There is a natural direct sum splitting

$$L_i^p(\mathbb{Z}\pi) = \bigoplus_{d \mid n} L_i^p(\mathbb{Z}\pi)(d)$$

such that

(i) $L_i^p(\mathbb{Z}\pi)(d)$ is mapped isomorphically under the restriction map to $L_i^p(\mathbb{Z}[\mathbb{Z}/d \rtimes \sigma])(d)$ and $L_i^p(\mathbb{Z}\pi)(d) = L_i^P(\mathbb{Z}\pi)(d)$ for $d > 1$.

(ii) There is an exact sequence for each $d \mid m$

$$\cdots \longrightarrow CL_{i+1}^K(S(d)) \longrightarrow L_i^P(\mathbb{Z}\pi)(d) \longrightarrow \prod_{p \nmid d} L_i^K(\hat{R}_p(d)) \oplus L_i^K(T(d))$$
$$\longrightarrow CL_i^K(S(d)) \longrightarrow \cdots$$

The improvement that has been made here is in the local term. Now if $p \nmid 2d$ and $\pi = \mathbb{Z}/d \rtimes \sigma$, the map

$$L_i^K(\hat{R}_p(d)) \longrightarrow L_i^K(\hat{S}_p(d))$$

splits according to the rational representations of π which are faithful on $\mathbb{Z}/d$. The remaining problem occurs for $p = 2$, and the map

$$(3.9) \qquad L_i^K(\hat{\mathbb{Z}}_2 \otimes \mathbb{Z}[\zeta_d]^t\sigma) \longrightarrow L_i^K(\hat{\mathbb{Q}}_2 \otimes \mathbb{Z}[\zeta_d]^t\sigma).$$

Remark. There is an analogue of (3.8) for $L_n^X(\mathbb{Z}\pi)(d)$ splitting (3.1), and again the only remaining "spreading" occurs at $p = 2$. The difference between L^X and $L^{\tilde{X}}$ occurs only at the d=1 component, and the geometrically significant groups $L^{\tilde{Y}}$ differ from $L^{\tilde{X}}$ by $H^*(\mathbb{Z}/2; \{\pm\pi^{ab}\})$. Note that on the d–component

$$H^*(\mathbb{Z}/2; \{\pm\pi^{ab}\})(d) = H^*(\mathbb{Z}/2; \{\pi^{ab}\})(d) = H^*(\mathbb{Z}/2; \{\sigma^{ab}\})$$

for $d \neq 1$. To obtain for example L^S from $L^{\tilde{Y}}$, we would still have to compute $H^*(\mathbb{Z}/2; SK_1(\mathbb{Z}\pi))$, although for example, it is known that this vanishes (and $L^S = L^{\tilde{Y}}$) when π has odd order. We will mostly concentrate on L^P for the rest of these lectures, in order to encounter as few K–theory complications as possible.

Example: As an application we prove the useful result of A.Bak that $L^?_{2k+1}(\mathbb{Z}\pi) = 0$ for π a group of odd order and $? = s$ or h.

By Dress induction, we may assume that $\pi = \mathbb{Z}/m$ is a cyclic of odd order m. For $d = 1$, we have

$$L_{2k+1}(\mathbb{Z}[\mathbb{Z}/m])(1) = L_{2k+1}(\mathbb{Z}) = 0,$$

by Kervaire–Milnor. For $d|m$ and $d > 1$, the factors of $S(d) = \mathbb{Q}(\zeta_d)$, $T(d) = \mathbb{R}(\zeta_d)$, and $\hat{R}_p(d)/J_p(d) = \mathbb{F}_p(\zeta_d)$ have non–trivial involution. Therefore $L_{2k+1} = 0$ for these factors, and (3.5) gives

$$(3.10) \qquad L^{\tilde{X}}_{2k+1}(\mathbb{Z}\pi) = L^X_{2k+1}(\mathbb{Z}\pi) = \prod_{\substack{d|m \\ d\neq 1}} L^{\hat{X}}_{2k+1}(\hat{\mathbb{Z}}_2[\zeta_d]).$$

But $L_n^K(\mathbb{F}_2[\zeta_d]) = 0$ for $d \neq 1$ and the difference between L^S and L^K is

$$H^*(\mathbb{Z}/2; K_1(\hat{\mathbb{Z}}_2[\zeta_d])).$$

Let $A = \hat{\mathbb{Z}}_2[\zeta_d]$ and consider the sequences

$$1 \longrightarrow (1+2A)^\times \longrightarrow A^\times \longrightarrow (A/2A)^\times \longrightarrow 1,$$

and

$$1 \longrightarrow (1+2^{r+1}A)^\times \longrightarrow (1+2^r A)^\times \xrightarrow{\ \ell\ } A/2A \longrightarrow 1,$$

for $r \geq 1$, where $\ell(1+2^r a) = a \pmod 2$. Since $(A/2A)^\times$ has odd order,

$$H^*(\mathbb{Z}/2; A^\times) = H^*(\mathbb{Z}/2; (1+2A)^\times),$$

and since $A/2A \cong \mathbb{F}_2[\zeta_d]$ has non–trivial involution,

$$H^*(\mathbb{Z}/2; (1+2^r A)^\times) = H^*(\mathbb{Z}/2; (1+2^{r+1}A)^\times).$$

It follows that $H^*(\mathbb{Z}/2; A^\times) = 0$ and so $L^{\tilde{X}}_{2k+1}(\mathbb{Z}\pi) = 0$ from (3.10).

Since m is odd, $L^s_{2k+1}(\mathbb{Z}\pi) \cong L^{\tilde{Y}}_{2k+1}(\mathbb{Z}\pi) \cong L^{\tilde{X}}_{2k+1}(\mathbb{Z}\pi) = 0$, and it remains to do L^h. The exact sequence

$$L^{\tilde{Y}}_{2k+1}(\mathbb{Z}\pi) \longrightarrow L^h_{2k+1}(\mathbb{Z}\pi) \longrightarrow H^1(\mathbb{Z}/2; Wh(\mathbb{Z}\pi)/SK_1(\mathbb{Z}\pi))$$

and the result of Wall that the Tate cohomology group vanishes (for any finite group π), finishes the proof.

Sources

I.Hambleton, A.A.Ranicki and L.Taylor,
"Round L–theory", J.of Pure and App. Alg. 47 (1987), 131–154.

E.K.Pedersen and A.A.Ranicki,
"Projective surgery theory", Topology 19 (1980), 2339–254.

A.A.Ranicki
"The algebraic theory of surgery I. Foundations", Proc. Lond.Math. Soc. (3) 40 (1980), 87–192.
" ______ II. Applications to topology", ibid., 193–283.

C.T.C.Wall,
"On the classification of hermitian forms II. Semisimple rings", Invent. Math. 18 (1972),119–141.
______ V. Adele rings", Invent.Math. 23 (1974),261–288

Lecture 4.

In this lecture we will describe the calculation of $L_i^p(\mathbb{Z}\pi)(d)$ for $\pi = \mathbb{Z}/d \rtimes \sigma$. We consider the exact sequence

$$(4.1) \qquad .. \longrightarrow L_{i+1}^p(\mathbb{Z}\pi \longrightarrow \hat{\mathbb{Z}}_2\pi) \longrightarrow L_i^p(\mathbb{Z}\pi) \longrightarrow L_i^h(\hat{\mathbb{Z}}_2\pi) \longrightarrow L_i^p(\mathbb{Z}\pi \longrightarrow \hat{\mathbb{Z}}_2\pi) \ldots$$

By (3.8) we have an exact sequence for the d–component

$$(4.2) \; .. \longrightarrow CL_{i+1}^K(S(d)) \longrightarrow L_{i+1}^p(\mathbb{Z}\pi \longrightarrow \hat{\mathbb{Z}}_2\pi)(d)$$

$$\longrightarrow \prod_{p \nmid 2d} L_i^K(\hat{R}_p(d)) \oplus L_i^K(T(d)) \xrightarrow{\gamma_i(d)} CL_i^K(S(d)) \longrightarrow \ldots$$

where each term and the maps split according to the decomposition of $S(d)$ into simple agebras. According to the discussion above we are reduced to the L–groups of (D,α,u) where D is a skew field with centre E, $\alpha\colon D \longrightarrow D$ is an anti–involution and $u = \pm 1$ is the symmetry of the forms. For E = finite field, $\mathbb{R}$ or $\mathbb{C}$, or a local field of characteristic $\neq 2$, the results are all classical. They depend on the usual types: **U, O, Sp** and **GL**, which can be determined from explicit character sum formulas. Since type GL makes no contribution to L–theory and O and Sp are interchanged by $(u \longrightarrow -u)$, we tabulate only type O and U. By type OK we mean $D = E$ and type OD, $D \neq E$.

<u>Table 1: E = local field</u>

(i) type U:	$L^K_{2i}(D) = H^0(E^\times), L^K_{2i+1}(D) = 0$
(ii) type OK:	$0 \longrightarrow \mathbb{Z}/2 \longrightarrow L^K_0(D) \longrightarrow H^0(E^\times) \longrightarrow 0$
	$L^K_1(D) = \mathbb{Z}/2,\ L^K_1(D) = L^K_1(D) = 0$
(iii) type OD:	$L^K_i(D) = \mathbb{Z}/2, 0,0,0 \quad (i{=}0,1,2,3 \bmod 4)$

<u>Table 2: E = ℝ or ℂ</u>

(i) type U:	$L^K_i(\mathbb{C},c,1) = 2\mathbb{Z}, 0, 2\mathbb{Z}, 0 \quad (i{=}0,1,2,3 \bmod 4)$
(ii) type O:	$L^K_i(\mathbb{R},1,1) = 2\mathbb{Z}, \mathbb{Z}/2, 0, 0$
	$L^K_i(\mathbb{C},1,1) = 0, \mathbb{Z}/2, 0, 0$
	$L^K_i(\mathbf{H},c,1) = 0, 0, 2\mathbb{Z}, 0.$

(If $\mathbf{H} = \mathbb{R}[i,j,k]$, then $c(i) = i$, $c(j) = j$ and $c(k) = -k$).

<u>Table 3: E = finite field</u>

(i) type U:	$L^K_i = 0$
(ii) type O:	$L^K_i(\mathbb{F}_q) = \mathbb{Z}/2, \mathbb{Z}/2, 0, 0 \quad (q \text{ odd})$
	$L^K_i(\mathbb{F}_q) = \mathbb{Z}/2, \mathbb{Z}/2, \mathbb{Z}/2, \mathbb{Z}/2 \quad (q{=}2^r).$

<u>Remark</u>: For E local, the L–groups are detected by the discriminant

$$L^K_i(D) \longrightarrow H^i(E^\times)$$

except in type OK. There the kernel of the discriminant is detected by the Hasse invariant. For $E = \mathbb{R}$ or $\mathbb{C}$, the L^K_{2i} are detected by the signature and L^K_1 by the discriminant. For $E = \mathbb{F}_q$, q odd, the groups are again detected by the discriminant. Finally, $L^K_{2i}(\mathbb{F}_{2^r})$ is detected by the Arf invariant, and $L^K_{2i+1}(\mathbb{F}_{2^r})$ is generated by the automorphism $\begin{pmatrix}0&1\\1&0\end{pmatrix}$. A tabulation for $L^s_i(D)$ in these three cases may be found in [Wall, VI].

The difficult part of sequence (4.2) is the term CL^K_i. If D is a skew field with centre a global field E, $D_A = D\otimes\hat{\mathbb{Q}} \oplus D\otimes\mathbb{R}$ denotes the adelic completion of D. Then we let $C(D) = K_1(D_A)/K_1(D)$. By weak approximation, $C(D) = C(E) = E^\times_A/E^\times$. The cobordism definition (3.4) of $CL^U_i(D)$ leads to an exact comparison sequence

(4.3) $$\longrightarrow H^{i+1}(C(E)) \xrightarrow{\delta} CL^S_i(D) \longrightarrow CL^K_i(D) \longrightarrow H^i(C(E)) \longrightarrow \dots .$$

The calculation of $CL^s_i(D)$ involves Galois cohomology and there is a "reciprocity law" in type O:

$$0 \longrightarrow L^s_0(D) \longrightarrow L^s_0(D_A) \longrightarrow CL^s_0(D) \longrightarrow 0, \qquad CL^s_0(D) = \mathbb{Z}/2$$

More precisely, the composite

$$L^s_0(\hat{D}_p) \longrightarrow L^s_0(D_A) \longrightarrow CL^s_0(D) \cong \mathbb{Z}/2$$

is an isomorphism for p finite and onto for p an infinite real place where D splits. Using this, and Kneser's formula for $\ker(L^K_0(D) \longrightarrow L^K_0(D_A))$, one can show that the map δ in (4.3) for $i = 0 \pmod 4$ is zero in type OK and non–zero in type OD.

Table 4: $CL^K_i(D)$

	type OK	type OD	type U
i=3	0	0	0
i=2	0	0	$H^0(C(E))$
i=1	$H^1(C(E))$	$\ker(\delta: H^1(C(E)) \to \mathbb{Z}/2)$	0
i=0	$\mathbb{Z}/2 \rtimes H^0(C(E))$	$H^0(C(E))$	$H^0(C(E))$

By using the tables above and a bit of diagram chasing, we can completely tabulate the domain, range, kernel and cokernel of the map $\gamma_i(d)$ from (4.2). Then there is an (naturally split) exact sequence,

$$0 \longrightarrow \operatorname{cok} \gamma_i(d) \longrightarrow L^p_i(\mathbb{Z}\pi \longrightarrow \hat{\mathbb{Z}}_2\pi)(d) \longrightarrow \ker \gamma_{i-1}(d) \longrightarrow 0$$

determining the relative group.

To illustrate the method, let us do type OK where the centre field E is totally real (all factors in $\mathbb{Q}\pi$ are of this type for π a dihedral group). Let $A \subseteq E$ denote the ring of integers, and $\Gamma(E)$ the ideal class group defined by

$$1 \longrightarrow E^\times/A^\times \longrightarrow \hat{E}^\times/\hat{A}^\times \longrightarrow \Gamma(E) \longrightarrow 1.$$

Consider the diagram

$$\begin{array}{ccc} \prod_{p \nmid 2d} L^K_i(\hat{A}_p) \times L^K_i(E_\infty) & \xrightarrow{\gamma_i} & CL^K_i(E) \\ \downarrow & & \downarrow \\ H^i(\hat{A}^\times_{2d'}) \times H^i(E^\times_\infty) & \xrightarrow{\tilde{\gamma}_i} & H^i(C(E)) \end{array}$$

where $\hat{A}^{\times}_{2d'} = \prod_{p \nmid 2d} \hat{A}^{\times}_{p}$. We will also use the notation $\hat{A}^{\times}_{2d} = \prod_{p \mid 2d} \hat{A}^{\times}_{p}$. Since $\tilde{\gamma}_i$ has the same kernel and cokernel as the map

$$H^i(\hat{A}^{\times}_{2d'}) \times H^i(E^{\times}_{\infty}) \times H^i(E^{\times}) \longrightarrow H^i(E^{\times}_{A}),$$

we are led to consider

$$\begin{array}{ccccccccccc}
0 \to & \ker \tilde{\gamma}_0 & \longrightarrow & H^0(\hat{A}^{\times}_{2d'}) \times H^0(E^{\times}_{\infty}) \times H^0(E^{\times}) & \longrightarrow & H^0(E^{\times}_{A}) & \longrightarrow & \operatorname{cok} \tilde{\gamma}_0 & \longrightarrow & 0 \\
& \downarrow & & \downarrow & & \| & & \downarrow & & \\
0 \to & E^{(2)}/E^{\times 2} & \longrightarrow & H^0(\hat{A}^{\times}) \times H^0(E^{\times}_{\infty}) \times H^0(E^{\times}) & \longrightarrow & H^0(E^{\times}_{A}) & \longrightarrow & H^0(\Gamma(E)) & \longrightarrow & 0 \\
& \downarrow & & \downarrow & & & & & & \\
& H^0(\hat{A}^{\times}_{2d}) & = & H^0(\hat{A}^{\times}_{2d}) & & & & & &
\end{array}$$

Here $E^{(2)}$ denotes the elements of E with even valuation at all finite primes. From the above diagram we obtain,

$$0 \longrightarrow \ker \tilde{\gamma}_0 \longrightarrow E^{(2)}/E^{\times 2} \xrightarrow{\ \Phi\ } H^0(\hat{A}^{\times}_{2d}) \longrightarrow \operatorname{cok} \tilde{\gamma}_0 \longrightarrow H^0(\Gamma(E)) \longrightarrow 0. \tag{4.4}$$

In type OK, $CL^K_0(E)$ is an extension of $H^0(C(E))$ by $CL^s_0(E) = \mathbb{Z}/2$. But since E is totally real, and $L^K_0(\mathbb{R},1,1)$ surjects onto $CL^s_0(E)$, we have also found $\ker \gamma_0$ and $\operatorname{cok} \gamma_0$. A similar, but easier analysis gives $\ker \gamma_i = 0$ for $i \neq 0$, $\operatorname{cok} \gamma_i = 0$ for $i \neq 0,1$ and an exact sequence

$$0 \longrightarrow H^1(A^{\times}) \longrightarrow H^1(\hat{A}^{\times}_{2d}) \longrightarrow \operatorname{cok} \gamma_1 \longrightarrow 0. \tag{4.5}$$

Although our expression $\operatorname{cok} \gamma_0 = \operatorname{cok} \Phi \oplus H^0(\Gamma(E))$ is complicated, the answer is in terms of familar quantities in algebraic number theory. It is not too hard, using class field theory, to give a formula for the ranks of $\ker\gamma_0$ and $\operatorname{cok}\gamma_0$ (they are elementary abelian 2–groups). Let $\gamma^*(A,2d)$ denote the 2–rank of the strict class group of $A[1/2d]$.

Proposition. In type OK with E is totally real, $\ker\gamma_0$ has 2–rank $\gamma^*(A,2d)$ and $\operatorname{cok}\gamma_0$ has 2–rank $(\Sigma_{p|2d}\, g_p + \gamma^*(A,2d))$, where g_p is the number of primes in A over a rational prime p.

To complete the calculation of $L_i^p(\mathbb{Z}\pi)(d)$, we must compute

$$L_i^h(\hat{\mathbb{Z}}_2\pi)(d) \to L_i^p(\mathbb{Z}\pi \to \hat{\mathbb{Z}}_2\pi)(d).$$

After the discussion of the relative group, we see that this factors through the composite

$$\bar{\psi}_i\colon L_i^h(\hat{\mathbb{Z}}_2\pi)(d) \longrightarrow L_i^h(\hat{\mathbb{Q}}_2\pi)(d) \longrightarrow \operatorname{cok}\gamma_i. \tag{4.6}$$

After reducing modulo the radical,

$$L_i^h(\hat{\mathbb{Z}}_2\pi)(d) \cong L_i^K(\hat{\mathbb{Z}}_2\otimes\mathbb{Z}[\zeta_d]^t\sigma) \cong L_i^K(\mathbb{F}_2\otimes\mathbb{Z}[\zeta_d]^\sigma,\alpha,1)$$

Since $\mathbb{F}_2\otimes\mathbb{Z}[\zeta_d]^\sigma = g_2(\mathbb{F}_2(\zeta_d)^\sigma)$, we get a direct sum of $g_2(\mathbb{Z}/2)$ for the domain of ψ_i provided that the anti–structure has type **O**. For the range of $\bar{\psi}_i$ we can use Table 1, combined with the character theory of π.

The irreducible complex characters of $\mathbb{Z}/d \rtimes \sigma$ which are faithful on $\mathbb{Z}/d$ are induced up from $\chi\otimes\xi$ on $\mathbb{Z}/d\times\sigma_1$ where $\sigma_1 = \ker(t\colon\sigma \longrightarrow (\mathbb{Z}/d)^\times)$. We say that ξ is a cyclic character of σ_1 if it is the pull–back of a character on a cyclic quotient. The anti–structure $(\mathbb{F}_2\otimes\mathbb{Z}[\zeta_d]^\sigma,\alpha,1)$ above has type **O** if and only if there is $g_0\in\sigma$ with $t(g_0) = -1$. If we scale the antistructure on $\hat{\mathbb{Z}}_2\otimes\mathbb{Z}[\zeta_d]^t\sigma = \hat{R}_2(d)$ by g_0 we get

$$\beta_0(g) = g_0 g^{-1} g_0^{-1}$$

and new unit $b_0 = g_0^2$. We say that ξ is a cyclic type **O** character if it is cyclic and type **O** in the antistructure $(\mathbb{Z}_2 \otimes \mathbb{Z}[\zeta_d]\sigma_1, \beta_0, b_0)$. A <u>twisted</u> cyclic character ξ of σ_1 is a cyclic character of order 2^ℓ with $\xi(b_0^{2^{\ell-1}}) = -1$.

<u>Theorem</u>. The map ψ_i in (4.6) is injective or zero. It is injective if and only if there is $g_0 \in \sigma$ with $t(g_0) = -1$ and one of the following holds

(a) for $i \equiv 0,1 \pmod 4$, there is a cyclic type **O** character.

(b) for $i \equiv 2,3 \pmod 4$, there is a cyclic type **Sp** character.

(c) for $i \equiv 0 \pmod 2$ there is a twisted cyclic type **U** character.

For the standard antistructure, it turns out that $\operatorname{cok} \gamma_i = 0$ in type **U** and so (c) does not affect the image of $\overline{\psi}_i$. When ψ_i is injective, its image is the projection (for the factor with centre E) of

$$\prod_{p|2} \langle -1 \rangle_p \in H^1(\hat{A}_{2d}^{\times}) \text{ or } \prod_{p|2} \langle 1-4\delta \rangle_p \in H^0(\hat{A}_{2d}^{\times})$$

into $\operatorname{cok} \gamma_1(E)$ or $\operatorname{cok} \Phi_E$ respectively ($\langle 1-4\delta \rangle$ is the 2–adic unit with minimal quadratic defect). See (4.4) and (4.5) for the relevant exact sequences. Of course to obtain an actual formula for $L_i^p(\mathbb{Z}\pi)(d)$ some more number theory must be done.

<u>Sources</u>

I.Hambleton and I.Madsen,
"On the computation of projective surgery obstruction groups", preprint (1987).
"On the discriminants of forms with Arf invariant one", preprint (1987).

I.Hambleton, L.Taylor and B.Williams,
"An introduction to the maps between surgery obstruction groups". <u>Algebraic Topology, Aarhus 1982</u>, 49–127, Lecture Notes in Mathematics 1051. Springer–Verlag, Berlin–Heidelberg–New York, 1984.

C.T.C.Wall,
"On the classification of hermitian forms.V1: Group rings". Ann. of Math. 103 (1976), 1–80.

Lecture 5.

The outcome of our program for calculating the surgery obstruction groups is still unsatisfactory. At best, the L–group is determined only up to extensions and the answer for the pieces is given in terms of (in general almost uncomputable) ideal class groups. Even worse is the fact that we have not seen any method to examine a particular element, for example the surgery obstruction of a normal map, within this complicated algebra.

If we concentrate now on the problem of determining whether a surgery obstruction is zero or non–zero, there are two important advances to be made. The first is an improvement on the Dress induction theorem. We define a basic 2–hyperelementary group to be one in which every normal abelian subgroup is cyclic. In [H–T–W] we classified these groups and proved that $\pi = \mathbb{Z}/d \rtimes \sigma$ is basic if and only if $\sigma_1 = \ker t$ is cyclic, semidihedral, quaternion, or dihedral (and if $\sigma_1 = D_8$, the map $\sigma \to \mathrm{Out}(D_8)$ is onto). Let

$$\bar{\pi} = \mathbb{Z}/d \rtimes (\sigma/[\sigma_1,\sigma_1])$$

and note that for any subquotient $(N \lhd H \subseteq \pi)$, there is a generalized restriction map $L^p_n(\mathbb{Z}\pi) \to L^p_n(\mathbb{Z}[H/N])$. Here we are assuming the standard oriented involution, although the following results can be extended to the non–orientable case.

Theorem 5.1. Let π be a 2–hyperelementary group. Then the sum of all the generalized restriction maps

$$L^p_n(\mathbb{Z}\pi) \to L^p_n(\mathbb{Z}[\bar{\pi}]) \oplus \sum \left\{ L^p_n(\mathbb{Z}[H/N]) \colon H/N \text{ is a basic subquotient of } \pi \right\}$$

is an injection.

The effect of this is to concentrate attention on the essential cases.

The second result we wish to mention concerns the detection of surgery obstructions $\lambda(f,b) \in L_n^p(\mathbb{Z}\pi)$ arising from a degree 1 normal map

$$(f,b)\colon M^n \longrightarrow X.$$

In this situation, there are certain primary invariants: the multi-signature, Arf invariants, semi-characteristic, and (cohomology) finiteness obstruction $\sigma_*(X) \in H^{n+1}(\tilde{K}_0(\mathbb{Z}\pi))$. In addition, on the kernel of the primary invariants, we have the δ-invariant:

$$\delta(f,b) \in H^{n+1}(Wh(\hat{\mathbb{Q}}_2\pi)/Wh'(\mathbb{Z}\pi))/\left\{L_{n+1}^h(\hat{\mathbb{Z}}_2\pi) \oplus d^* H^n(\tilde{K}_0(\mathbb{Z}\pi))\right\}.$$

<u>Theorem 5.2</u>. For any oriented degree 1 normal map (f,b), the projective surgery obstruction $\lambda(f,b)$ is detected by the multisignature, Arf invariants, semicharacteristic, cohomology finiteness obstruction and the δ-invariant.

The surgery semicharacteristic $\chi_{\frac{1}{2}}(f,b) \in L_{2k+1}^h(\hat{\mathbb{Z}}_2\pi)$ is defined as follows. Since $\hat{\mathbb{Z}}_2\pi/J_2\pi = A$ is a semisimple ring, $L_{2k+1}^p(A) = 0$ and $L_{2k+1}^h(A)$ can be identified with a quotient of $\tilde{K}_0(A)$, via the sequence

$$\longrightarrow L_{2k+2}^p(A) \longrightarrow H^1(\tilde{K}_0(A)) \longrightarrow L_{2k+1}^h(A) \longrightarrow 0.$$

Then

$$\chi_{\frac{1}{2}}(f,b) = \chi_{\frac{1}{2}}(M;A) - \chi_{\frac{1}{2}}(X;A)$$

where

$$\chi_{\frac{1}{2}}(X;A) = \sum_{i=0}^{k} (-1)^k [H_i(X;A)] \in \tilde{K}_0(A).$$

The semi–characteristic gives the image of $\lambda(f,b)$ in $L^h_{2k+1}(\hat{\mathbb{Z}}_2\pi)$ under the natural map.

Similarly, the other primary invariants give the images of $\lambda(f,b)$:

$\mathrm{sign}(f,b) \in L^h_n(\mathbb{R}\pi)$,

$A(f,b) \in L^h_{2k}(\hat{\mathbb{Z}}_2\pi)$, and

$\sigma_*(X) \in H^{n+1}(\tilde{K}_0(\mathbb{Z}\pi))$.

The δ–invariant is defined by an additive relation

$$\begin{array}{ccccc}
L^h_n(\mathbb{Z}\pi) & \longrightarrow & L^U_n(\hat{\mathbb{Z}}_2\pi) & \longleftarrow & H^{n+1}(Wh'(\hat{\mathbb{Z}}_2\pi)/Wh'(\mathbb{Z}\pi)) \\
\downarrow & & & & \downarrow \\
L^p_n(\mathbb{Z}\pi) & & \dashrightarrow^{\delta} & & H^{n+1}(Wh(\hat{\mathbb{Q}}_2\pi)/Wh'(\mathbb{Z}\pi))
\end{array}$$

where $U = \mathrm{Im}(Wh'(\mathbb{Z}\pi) \rightarrow Wh'(\hat{\mathbb{Z}}_2\pi))$.

The proof of (5.2) is obtained by considering the diagram (with $V = Wh'(\hat{\mathbb{Z}}_2\pi)/U$):

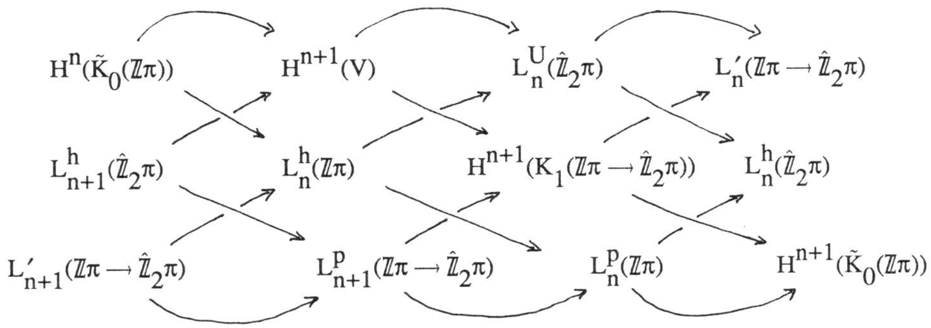

Finally we will briefly indicate how the δ–invariant may be computed. The arithmetic sequence in K–theory

$$0 \longrightarrow \mathrm{Wh}(\mathbb{Q}\pi)/\mathrm{Wh}'(\mathbb{Z}\pi) \longrightarrow \mathrm{Wh}(\hat{\mathbb{Q}}\pi)/\mathrm{Wh}'(\hat{\mathbb{Z}}\pi) \xrightarrow{\partial} \tilde{K}_0(\mathbb{Z}\pi) \longrightarrow 0$$

leads to an exact sequence in Tate cohomology

$$0 \longrightarrow \frac{H^{n+1}(\mathrm{Wh}(\mathbb{Q}\pi)/\mathrm{Wh}'(\mathbb{Z}\pi))}{d^* H^n(\tilde{K}_0(\mathbb{Z}\pi))} \xrightarrow{j_*} H^{n+1}(\mathrm{Wh}(\hat{\mathbb{Q}}\pi)/\mathrm{Wh}(\hat{\mathbb{Z}}\pi)) \xrightarrow{\partial_*} H^{n+1}(\tilde{K}_0(\mathbb{Z}\pi)).$$

Now if C is an algebraic Poincaré n–complex of f.g. projective $\mathbb{Z}\pi$–modules, there is an idelic torsion invariant

$$\hat{\Delta}(C,h) \in K_1(\hat{\mathbb{Q}}\pi)/K_1(\hat{\mathbb{Z}}\pi),$$

where h is a base for $H_*(C)$ compatible with Poincaré duality. If $C = C_*(X)$ where X is a finitely–dominated space, then $\partial\hat{\Delta}(C,\mathbf{h}) = \sigma(X)$ is the finiteness obstruction of X. If C is a finite free complex, then $j\Delta(C,\mathbf{h}) = \hat{\Delta}(C,\mathbf{h})$ where $\Delta(C,\mathbf{h})$ is the ordinary Reidemeister torsion of C. If C is a Poincaré complex, then the cohomology class

$$\{\hat{\Delta}(C,h)\} \in H^{n+1}(\mathrm{Wh}(\hat{\mathbb{Q}}\pi)/\mathrm{Wh}(\hat{\mathbb{Z}}\pi))$$

is defined and independent of the choice of h. Therefore, if X is a finitely dominated Poincaré complex with $\sigma_*(X) = 0$, we have a well–defined invariant

$$\Delta_0(X) \in \frac{H^{n+1}(\mathrm{Wh}(\mathbb{Q}\pi)/\mathrm{Wh}'(\mathbb{Z}\pi))}{d^* H^n(\tilde{K}_0(\mathbb{Z}\pi))}.$$

Notice that there is a natural map i_* from the domain of $\Delta_0(X)$ to the domain of the δ–invariant.

Theorem. For a degree 1 normal map $(f,b) : M^n \longrightarrow X$ with $\sigma_*(X) = 0$, and $\chi_{\frac{1}{2}}(f,b) = 0$ (n odd) or $A(f,b) = 0$ (n even),

$$\delta(f,b) = i_*(\Delta_0(M) - \Delta_0(X)).$$

We conclude with a geometric result, that was proved using some of the techniques discussed in these lectures (see [H–M]). Consider a semi–free topological action of a finite group π on $\mathbb{R}^{n+k}$ with fixed point set $\mathbb{R}^k$. Then π acts freely on $\mathbb{R}^{n+k} - \mathbb{R}^k = S^{n-1} \times \mathbb{R}^{k+1}$ and so must be a group with periodic cohomology. A particularly interesting class of such groups are the groups

$$Q(8a,b) = \mathbb{Z}/ab \rtimes Q_8$$

where a,b are coprime integers and the centralizer of $\mathbb{Z}/ab$ has index 4. These groups have a free linear representation in dimensions 8ℓ ($\ell \geq 1$) but none in any other dimension, so it is clear that π acts semi–freely on $(\mathbb{R}^{8\ell},0)$ or $(\mathbb{R}^{8\ell+k},\mathbb{R}^k)$, but unclear whether π acts on $(\mathbb{R}^{8\ell+4},0)$.

To answer this question, we let $A = \mathbb{Z}[\eta_a,\eta_b]$ and $E = \mathbb{Q}[\eta_a,\eta_b]$ where $\eta_a = \zeta_a + \zeta_a^{-1}$. Then

$$\Phi_E : E^{(2)} \longrightarrow H^0((A/ab)^\times)$$
$$\varphi_E : E^{(2)} \longrightarrow H^0((A/4A)^\times) \cong A/2A$$

are the reduction maps. For integers α and a, $\alpha \| a$ means that α is a full prime power divisor of a. Let

$$v_p(a) = \prod \{2 - \eta_\alpha : \alpha \| ab \text{ and } (\alpha,p) = 1\}$$

for each rational prime $p \mid a$. Next let

$$v(a) = \{v_p(a) : p \mid a\} \in \prod_{p \mid a} (A/p)^\times \cong (A/a)^\times$$

and similarly for $v(b)$.

Let

$$V(a,b) = (-1)^{r+1}(v(a),v(b)) \in H^0((A/ab)^\times)$$

where r is the number of rational prime divisors of ab.

Theorem ([H–M]). The group $\pi = Q(8a',b')$ acts semi–freely on $(\mathbb{R}^{8\ell+4},0)$ if and only if $V(a,b)$ is in the image of Φ_E restricted to the kernel of φ_E for each subgroup $Q(8a,b)$ of π.

We remark that the quantity $V(a,b)$ is essentially the idelic torsion of a Poincaré complex model for the action. The (ab)–component of $L_3^Y(\hat{\mathbb{Z}}_2\pi)$ contains $A/2A$ and $\varphi_E(\Phi_E^{-1}(V(a,b)))$ is the δ–invariant of a suitable normal map.

Sources

J.F.Davis,
"The surgery semicharacteristic", Proc.Lond.Math. Soc. (3) 47 (1983), 411–428.

I.Hambleton and I.Madsen,
"Actions of finite groups on $\mathbb{R}^{n+k}$ with fixed set $\mathbb{R}^k$, Canadian J.Math. 38 (1986), 781–860.

I.Hambleton, L.Taylor and B.Williams,
"Detection theorems in K and L–theory", preprint (1987).

R.Lee,
"Semicharacteristic classes", Topology 12 (1973), 183–199.

Department of Mathematics
McMaster University
Hamilton, Ontario,
CANADA